A Framework for Reading

Creating a Policy in the Elementary School

Muriel Somerfield
Mike Torbe
Colin Ward

for the City of Coventry Local Education Authority

North American adaptation and new material
Arlene M. Pillar

HEINEMANN
PORTSMOUTH, N.H.

Heinemann Educational Books Inc.
70 Court Street, Portsmouth, New Hampshire 03801

LONDON   EDINBURGH   MELBOURNE   AUCKLAND
HONG KONG   SINGAPORE   KUALA LUMPUR
NEW DELHI   IBADAN   NAIROBI   JOHANNESBURG
KINGSTON   PORT OF SPAIN

© City of Coventry Local Education Authority 1983, 1985
© North American adaptation and new material Arlene M. Pillar 1985
First published 1985
ISBN 0-435-08218-3

Library of Congress Cataloging in Publication Data

Somerfield, Muriel.
A framework for reading.

Bibliography: p.
Includes index.
1. Reading (Elementary) 2. Children—Books and
reading. I. Torbe, Mike. II. Ward, Colin.
III. Pillar, Arlene M. IV. Coventry (West Midlands,
England). Local Education Authority. V. Title.
LB1573.S78 1985   372.4   85-5603
ISBN 0-435-08218-3

Printed in the United States of America

Contents

A Note about the Adaptation

Books worthy of adaptation are outstanding books with important ideas which deserve to be made available to a broader audience than was first intended. It is never easy to adapt such books for fear of excluding information that should be included. In adapting *A Framework for Reading*, I have tried to use a nearly invisible hand. There were difficult decisions regarding the text's organization: two chapters were merged, and a new one—"The Librarian in the Reading Program"— was added. While it was easy to change "favourite" to "favorite" and "headteacher" to "principal," it was not so easy to locate replacement quotations for those from the Bullock Report, a planned aspect of the adaptation which was finally abandoned. Adding children's books published in North America was only mildly herculean, but there are so many wonderful books available today that some "old friends" had to be omitted in the interest of space.

Although the task of an adaptor is not to be envied, the labor of this adaptor was most pleasant due largely to the opportunity of working with Philippa Stratton, the consummate editor. I am indebted to Bernice Cullinan, dear friend and mentor, for more than I can say. I am grateful to Muriel Somerfield, Mike Torbe, and Colin Ward for the chance to bring their important work to this side of the Atlantic.

Arlene M. Pillar
Long Beach, New York, 1985

A Framework for Reading

Introduction

If there was one central idea in the Bullock Report, *A Language for Life,* that caught people's interest, it was the idea of a language policy. The request that every school should have an "organized policy for language across the curriculum" was originally met in various ways. Some local authorities very quickly published definitive documents whose apparent intention was that the "policy" was embodied in the document and could be quickly implemented in the school. The assumption was that a language policy was something external which exists, which can be written down, and can then be taken over and put into practice by a school.

Our own belief is different. We believe that a language policy is the internal construct of a school, constructed through dialogue about the teaching of all aspects of language. It is through such dialogue that a school can "devise a systematic policy for the development of reading competence in pupils of all ages and ability levels" which was one of the Bullock Committee's principal recommendations. A staff which sets out to discuss its whole approach to the teaching of language, though, needs some kind of framework to support and maintain the discussion. This book had its origins in our attempt to provide a starting point, or more accurately, a set of starting points, for such discussion.

The early version of the *Framework,* called "Towards a language policy: a discussion paper on reading for heads and staff" began by identifying issues about the teaching of reading and then asking questions which would act as discussion starters for schools. They were questions with no final, once-and-for-all answers: the answers change as circumstances, staff, children and resources change. Therefore, to define and construct a policy, a staff should recognize that they will need to conduct a constant dialogue about the issues that the questions raise. Most teachers already face and solve the problems naturally in their day-to-day work; but to be a "policy" each person's answer must be made explicit rather than remain unspoken, and then the separate answers brought together in a collaborative decision about what is to be done.

Asking questions, though, is the easiest part of constructing a policy: it is finding the answers which is difficult. This book, therefore, proposes a framework for the individual, or the school. It is a collection of good practice, based on the work of teachers who shared with the authors their experiences and expertise. It is intended to help with the day-to-day business of teaching reading, so the chapters contain approaches which have been tried and found successful. But the approaches are more than successful "tips": they are also related to implicit principles about the teaching of reading.

A school which wants to sort out its own approach to reading must make its principles explicit. The writers of this book have their own beliefs about reading, on which the book is based. They believe these things about reading:

that the teaching of reading should not be a barrier to children's enjoyment of books.

that involving children with real books from the beginning is the best way of developing good attitudes to reading.

that whatever we do in the teaching of reading it must have as its main purpose the *enjoyment* of reading.

that some methods of teaching reading can kill all desire to read.

that reading is not about "practicing skills"; it should always have a real purpose.

that once reading becomes an exercise, it ceases to be real reading.

that the language of early books should be as natural as possible.

that classroom organizations which help teachers don't always help learners.

that different children need to be taught to read in different ways.

that choice in reading is important.

that the choice of books should be based on what children actually like and enjoy, rather than our choice of what we feel they *ought* to read.

The book does not pretend to be a complete manual for the teaching of reading. The first chapter proposes one approach to the teaching of reading, and the last chapter considers the difficult question of assessment. The other chapters deal with areas which seem to us to be the most common causes of concern for teachers.

One area which is not directly dealt with is the teaching of reading to minority groups. There are two reasons for this. We believe that the principles defined above and the practice described in the main body by the book apply to *all* children, and so are appropriate for every school, whatever its population. Secondly, the central intention of the book is to offer a framework, and that means its contents must, as far as possible, be universal. It is up to each individual school to interpret them and apply them to its own peculiar context.

Because this is now a published book, many readers will use the book in their own private ways rather than as a staff discussion document. But the book may still, we hope, help administrators and teachers to synthesize their varied experiences into a common set of beliefs and classroom practice, appropriate to their own school. That is the only real way to construct a reading policy.

1

The Teaching of Reading: A General Approach

All experienced teachers know that:

different children work in different ways.

to help all children a teacher needs various approaches.

It would therefore be wrong to suppose that any one method can be used to teach all children to read. If there is only one method being used in a school then, whatever it is, some children will not manage to learn to read.

We believe that an improvement in the teaching of reading will not come about from the acceptance of simplistic statements about phonics or any other single aspect of reading, but from a comprehensive study of all the factors at work and the influence that can be exerted upon them.

A Language for Life: The Bullock Report (6.3)

Relationships Between Letters and Sounds

The beginning reader has to learn that words in books represent the sounds and meanings of the spoken language.

In the early stages of teaching reading, it is important to recognize that children already "know" things about language. To help them to understand the relationship between letter and sound, their early reading experience should build on what is already familiar:

stories written in familiar language make the best material for reading to (and with) children.

key words and phrases in the text can be pointed out. For example:

with "joining-in" stories follow with a finger the words the children are saying.

focus attention on the words which are to come on this page or the next one: pause before turning to that page or reading the words out.

provide tapes of stories and the text so that children can follow the story in the book while they are listening.

Simple activities like these help children to learn that this set of symbols represents this word and these meanings.

Decoding

The poorest readers are those who read word by word, even letter by letter.

The best are those who are not conscious of "reading words" at all, and use context and meaning before they use word analysis.

"Decoding," therefore, is best dealt with in the context of reading for meaning, rather than in separate exercises.

A child who has read "clock" correctly may hesitate lower down on the page over "closed." Two possible ways of dealing with this are:

tell the child what the word is, so as not to interfere with the reading for meaning.

ask the child to read on and guess the word, basing the guess on the context.

Whichever one uses, after the reading point back to the two words, and draw the reader's attention to the "cl-" they have in common. This seems to be more effective than showing the learner the pattern "cl-" in isolation.

The game "My aunt went to town" can be played in ways that are helpful. As each child adds a word to the list ("My aunt went to town and bought a clock/some clothes/a clarinet . . .") the teacher writes them on the board, so that whoever is next can read them off.

Ability to Anticipate What Comes Next

The ability to ask, and answer, the question "What comes next?" is crucial in learning to read. It is generally agreed that the ability to anticipate is a basic element in reading. Without realizing it, readers constantly guess ahead and then modify those guesses in the light of what they actually read. If readers concentrate on individual words, they cannot hold enough of the meaning to be aware of what they are reading; so they cannot predict what will happen next. When readers are able to predict, it is because they understand what has happened so far in whatever they are reading. Asking them to predict helps them to develop the idea that they need to know what *has* happened, in order to say what happens next. The following strategies apply to young learners:

While reading a book to a child or class, pause and ask, "What do you think will happen next?" No comment should be made about the suggestions, but when you have read on, ask the children to think back to what they thought would happen, and what they now think will happen. This can be used not only while reading the story but also when showing the pictures.

Use group prediction and group sequencing activities (with or without pictures). (See p. 97 for a description.)

Use cloze procedure to involve prediction and anticipation.

Invite small groups of children to discuss (not to write) how they think a story will continue after hearing the first part. They can be asked to make explicit to you, or to other children, what the clues were that they used to make their decision. After the discussion, complete the story.

Show the children a picture and ask them what the text is likely to be about. This can also be done by presenting a picture and asking the children to write (preferably in small groups) the text to go with it. Then show them the original which may be a picture from a book, or a newspaper picture, for example.

It is significant that at the stage when children first become efficient readers, they very often turn to the last pages of the book to see what happens. Presumably one thing they are doing is looking for the final clue which will help to make sense of the smaller clues along the way. The more complex the book, the more the reader needs to predict and anticipate what will happen next.

Flexible Reading Strategies

By "flexible reading strategies" is meant the reader's ability to adjust to different reading materials in appropriate ways. This includes skimming and scanning as well as concentrated purposeful reading. It is important to note that 5- and 6-year-olds who are using information books can also be introduced to all these strategies.

The reader needs to know why a piece of reading is being undertaken. Where information is being sought, questions are best asked *before* the passage is read.

Give out questions before you give out the passage. Ask the children to discuss the questions and come to tentative answers before they see the passage.

Give out the questions one at a time, without telling the children where the answer will be found. After all the questions have been answered, ask the children how they read the passage to find the answers. You can introduce thus the idea of skimming and scanning, and of searching for key words.

Use one piece of material to demonstrate the various purposes for which one can read. For instance, using *TV Guide,* one could ask:

How many children's programs are there today?

In what program does _ _ _ _ _ _ _ _ appear? (name a current personality)

What is tonight's Midnight Movie about?

Which program tells you about ostriches, and what surprising things does the article in TV Guide *say about them?*

How was the program made that's on CBS at 8:30?

It is important to use a current copy of *TV Guide,* not a word sheet. Otherwise you will have done all the skimming and scanning for them.

Fluent Reading—Extracting Meaning from the Printed Page

Unless children are "extracting meaning from the printed page," they cannot be said to be reading. From the beginning, then, they should be helped to see how important that is. At a simple level, this can be done with any book by asking:

What had happened when we stopped reading last time?

Tell me some of the things that happened in the book you have just read.

Which parts did you like best?

Tell other children what the book you've just read was about.

Children who have just started reading should always be invited to make sense of what they are reading.

Write messages to children (on the blackboard or on a card) without reading them aloud. The messages should be ones to be acted upon—

Who wants to borrow The Wreck of the Zephyr? *Come and ask if you do.*

Remind me to switch on the tape recorder at 10:15.

If you want me to read to you, bring me a book you want to hear.

Give instructions on paper for a coming event.

Put children together in small groups of three to five, with a tape recorder, to talk about one book they have all read.

for fiction: "Talk about the book and especially about the parts you enjoyed most."

for poetry: "Talk about the poem and anything else it made you think about."

for nonfiction: "Talk about the book and especially anything new you've learned from it."

Invite children to choose the part that they enjoyed most, and read it to each other.

NOTE that it is very difficult for children to "extract meaning" from some reading series books, because they do not tell a story.

A Policy for Hearing Children Read

Independence in Reading

The aim in teaching reading is to produce *independent readers.* By this is meant readers who will:

choose reading as an activity.

read with understanding those texts within their grasp.

struggle to derive meaning from more difficult texts.

be able to use books to search for information.

What teachers do while hearing children read should help them to move toward independence.

Making a Start

If children are beginning a new book, it is useful to do any or all of these: they all introduce the idea that everything in a book is relevant to its meaning. The teacher can:

discuss the title and the cover picture.

ask the child to guess what the book will be about.

read some of the book to the child as a sample.

perhaps even read the whole book first to a group of children, so that they have a clear idea of the story and language of this new book.

flip through it with the children, looking at the pictures and guessing what the pictures are about to introduce the idea of browsing.

If the child has already been reading this book, establish what point was reached:

refer to the events of the book, not to page numbers. Thus, say "We'd just reached the part where the little bird had built the nest . . ."

if the child has continued reading between reading sessions with the teacher, ask, "Where did you get to without me?" and expect not to be shown, but to be told about the intervening part.

Miscues

K. and Y. Goodman (1973) propose that "errors" should be seen not as mistakes to be corrected, but as *miscues,* which should be analyzed, because they demonstrate how a reader tackles print, and what particular strategy is being used by this reader. Smith (1971) suggests that children produce the most incomprehensible errors when they have no understanding of what they are reading.

When children are having difficulty in reading, then the principles to guide our response should be:

to learn from their error, and respond to what they are trying to do.

to make sure at all times that the concentration is on understanding the meaning and *not* on accuracy. Accuracy is only valuable if it helps the reader to understand better.

Making Meaning

There are children who correctly say every word on a page but do not derive meaning from the text. These children need to be identified because their problem will not show up on a word-recognition test: indeed, they may score high, because the test does not examine understanding. Some reasons for this apparent inability to understand are:

the children's unfamiliarity with the spoken language; this would apply, for example, to children whose mother tongue is not English.

difficulties in the text, caused by a mismatch between the language and experience of the children, and that which the text offers: the difficulties involve unfamiliar language patterns, and words and ideas outside the children's experience.

children who do not understand that words in books tell a story or at least mean something.

These problems are not easily solved, but if the teacher consistently emphasizes the meaning of the text, the children will gradually learn to understand what they read.

The Place of Phonics

Children sometimes use their existing knowledge of sounds to work out a word. If they do this and get it right, let them continue. But if they cannot correctly construe words, move them away from a phonic approach, and encourage them to use context and meaning.

It is sometimes useful for the teacher to use a phonic approach herself in saying words, to demonstrate their structure.

If children are asked to sound out words they have difficulty with, they can be slowed down so that they lose the meaning of the text.

Helping the Hesitant Reader

When the reader hesitates, remains silent, or makes a miscue, choose from among these approaches, all of which emphasize meaning.

In General

Wait. Given time, without being put under pressure, children will often show that they were working it out successfully.

If, however, the reader is hesitating a great deal, then supply the word. Too much hesitation means that the meaning of the text will be lost because the reader will forget what went before.

If the Child Supplies the Wrong Word

Let the reader carry on to the end of the sentence, or paragraph, and then ask, "Does that word make sense there?"

Occasionally, ask the reader to reread the sentence. Sometimes, because they are now carrying the meaning of the whole sentence, children correct themselves.

Ask the child to reread the sentence, but supply the word previously read wrongly, as soon as the reader reaches it.

Reread the sentence, pausing for the child to supply the word.

In all cases, the reader is being encouraged to use meaning and context to solve the miscue.

If the Child Remains Silent

Ask the reader to guess what the word might be, using the rest of the text, the picture, or anything else that might help. Then check back at the end of the sentence to see if it still seems right.

Draw the child's attention to parts of the word that might be familiar. For instance, "downstairs" might be difficult; but the reader will probably recognize "down" if "stairs" is covered, and be able to construct the whole word.

Reread the sentence up to the problem word. Sometimes

hearing the sentence read fluently shows the child what it means; and it is then possible to supply the missing word.

General Principles

Enjoyment The time that teacher and child spend together should be pleasurable for both. The aim is to make the story, or whatever is being read, as interesting and enjoyable as possible for both parties.

A Special Time The children should know that they have the teacher's complete attention, and while they are reading together will have the time to enjoy it. They should sit somewhere where they both feel comfortable and at ease, and where they can give each other full attention.

Choice Although the book that is being read is often defined for the children by the reading series, they should sometimes have the chance to choose a book they want to read from. Children often like to reread a book, and also like to read "easy" books; or they may want to read nonfiction books to the teacher. They should have that chance.

Making Meaning The main energies of both teacher and child should be on making sense of the text, and not merely on accuracy or speed. So "reading time" should include time to talk about what has been read.

Allow Time Time in one block seems to work more effectively than the same amount of time spread out. Thus, it seems useful to allow children more time when they are actually reading, and to cut down the number of times per week when they come to the teacher. Two sessions of five minutes each per week are better than five of two minutes each, because in the longer span, the children can read more of the book, and take in more of the meaning (Southgate, 1982). Another way of creating time is for the children to be able to read into a tape recorder. The teacher can listen to the tape later, at leisure.

Demonstrate Reading If the teacher and child sometimes read paragraphs or pages alternately, children gain a better understanding of punctuation, learn how to use expression in the voice, are helped to give more meaning to the reading, and also see that the teacher values the experience, too.

Silent Reading Reading aloud to the teacher is only a stage on the way to independent reading, which is generally silent.

At all times, reading aloud should be mixed with encouragement to the children to read silently. Occasionally, one might ask a child to read the text silently before coming to the teacher; and then use the time together to *talk about* what has been read.

What Do You Record While Listening to Children Reading?

Observe particularly the following:

What words are hesitated over? Is there a pattern to them? If so, what is it?

Whether the child reads single words, like a list, or in phrases and sentences so they sound as if they mean something.

Whether the child observes punctuation and so is able to create the sound of a speaking voice. (Note, though, that this has more to do with satisfactory *performance* than with understanding. It is possible to read aloud fluently and to pay no attention to what one is reading.)

The speed of reading. Speed itself is not a virtue; but too fast or too slow both suggest lack of understanding. The speed of a reader can be classified usefully as:

slow listing —*that is, one word at a time*

halting —*two-three words at a time*

natural —*sounds like the speaking voice*

overly fluent—*too fast for meaning*

Whether the children follow with their finger. If children do this, or have a card underneath the line, they slow themselves down, because the eye is kept from its natural movement along the lines. They should be encouraged to take in at least four words at a time, and to say those while their eye is tracking to the next four. Instruct them in this technique by saying, "Look at the first few words without saying anything: then while you are saying them look at the next four words."

Whether the child's facial expressions show understanding. If the common expression on children's faces during reading is anxiety, they are unlikely to be learning much. Look for the smiles, frowns, nods and so on that demonstrate involvement.

What kind of book this child normally brings.

Whether the reader seems to have understood the passage or the whole book.

How Do You Check Whether the Children Have Understood?

Comprehension questions do not necessarily tell us if the reader has or has not understood the book or the text. They may only tell us if the questions themselves have been understood. Moreover, it is not always easy to find out if the children have understood the full meaning of a text, because it can be hard for readers of any age to put their understanding into words for others. A reader's understanding is more likely to be displayed in less obvious ways.

Talk with the child during, and especially after the reading of a book. Ask questions that will enable the reader to begin to talk about the book:

Which part did you enjoy best?

Was there any part you found hard?

Who did you like best?

Was there anyone you didn't like?

The reader's answers will give you an idea of the amount he or she has understood. More specific questions about parts of the text can be tried:

Why do you think he did this?

What did he mean when he said . . . ?

Invite them to relate the text to their own experience;

Have you seen or heard anything like that?

Has anything like that happened to you ever?

Invite the reader to guess what will happen next.

Invite a reader to come, after he or she has finished reading the book, and tell you what *did* happen.

Invite the child to read or tell the story onto tape. A told version, especially, will be very illuminating about what is and is not understood; but very young children may have difficulty in doing this.

Invite the child, with others who have read the same story, to dramatize some or all of it. Puppets seem to encourage children to put the story into words more than drama does.

How Do You Monitor a Child's Enjoyment of the Story?

This can only be done by careful observation:

in a group discussion with children who have all read the same book.

of appropriate responses during reading (see previous section).

if the reader chooses voluntarily to read other books by this author, or wants to reread this one.

However, negative responses are easier to detect: boredom, anxiety, even fear, all point to an absence of enjoyment.

How Do You Insure that Your Teaching of Reading Is Integrated with Your Teaching of Everything Else?

The most effective instruction occurs when the reading is serving the reader's immediate purposes, and not when reading is being taught in separate timetabled periods.

It seems to be generally agreed that "transfer of skills" very rarely occurs in reading: that is, if children are taught comprehension, skimming and scanning and so on, from exercises, there is no guarantee that they will use those abilities successfully when it comes to topic work.

Thus all areas of the curriculum should be used to encourage the development of reading. The examples that follow demonstrate ways of doing this.

When children are beginning a topic, make sure they draw up a list of questions to which they want to find answers; and they should also indicate on the list the kinds of books they will need to go to for the answers.

When answering questions, children will only develop the ability to locate and retrieve relevant information if the search for the book and page is an important part of the teaching program. They will not develop those abilities if they are always directed to individual books, or to identified pages or lines.

Occasionally choose a topic which will make sure that children meet an apparent confusion of information in different books—for instance, the life history of beavers, the reasons for the decline of dinosaurs. Help the children to compare and assess the information and to come to conclusions.

Encourage skimming and scanning at all times: "Find me the page in the math book where the problems were about parrots." "Can you find that picture of the nuclear explosion you showed me in this book?"

"There's a story in this book about ghosts; find it for me and I'll read it today."

Make time available for extended sustained reading, not only of stories but of "topic" books.

If children are likely to have problems with reading the page of a math book, make a tape or Language Master cards of the text so that children can play it and follow in the book. Thus they are being helped to do the math which is the main purpose, but following it in the text will also be teaching them to read.

Summary In broad terms, certain principles can be applied which will help to integrate the teaching of reading into general work:

When planning, be aware of all the times the children read in the course of the day. Plan so that the children extend and develop their ability to handle books.

When children have problems with reading in science, math, or other content areas, the problems need solving immediately, not later in "reading" lessons.

Insure that the books you select for your reference library are properly indexed.

The aim is that children should be able to locate and select appropriate books rather than being directed to a specific book.

2

Involving Parents with Reading

In a child's formative years, parental involvement can be crucial for learning to read. Children develop into more efficient readers where a mother or father is supportive during the early stages of reading. But children can become confused if the home and the school offer different counsel. The school can advise on the best ways of helping.

> It has been said that the way to prepare the very young child for reading is to hold him on your lap and read aloud to him stories he likes, over and over again. This is the most valuable piece of advice that a parent can be given.
> *A Language for Life: The Bullock Report (7.2)*

The question remains—how do we best tell parents about preparing their children for reading? There are two dimensions to this question:

When do you tell parents?
How can you organize the telling most effectively?

We suggest there are three groups of parents to be considered:

Preschool: those whose children are aged 0–3.
Prospective parents: those whose children will soon enter the nursery or elementary school.
Present parents: those whose children are in school already.

We also suggest five possible ways of making contact:

(i)   Informal group contact.
(ii) One-to-one contact.
(iii) Parent-to-parent contact.
(iv) Organized (formal) meeting.
(v)   Information sent home.

The following table summarizes a number of possible opportunities for formal and informal contact. Below and following are details of these activities, arranged in alphabetical order. It is not suggested that any one school would undertake all these suggestions. It is a list from which to select.

	i) Informal group contact	ii) One-to-one contact	iii) Parent-to-parent contact	iv) Organized (formal) meetings	v) Information sent home
Preschool (Children 0–3)	Coffee mornings Play-group attended by teacher Preschool group attended by teacher	Book stores Education store Education happening Home library Home visiting by administrator or teacher with materials		Video/film	Booklet about nursery school or nursery class Newsletter
Prospective (Nursery and Kindergarten 3–5)	Coffee mornings Discussion group in a home Discussion group in school Outings Open day Preschool group attended by teacher Social evening	Before or after formal meetings Fixed interviews Home visiting by reception teacher with preschool materials Home library/bookstore Invitations to 2, 3, 4 parents to visit classroom for afternoon Parents helping in school Phone conversations	Trained parents leading in pre-school sessions Trained parents visiting homes with preschool materials	Book fairs Preliminary visits to school Reading workshops Ready-for-school meetings Video/film	Booklets on reading School brochure School magazine
Present (Children already in school 5+)	Arranged visits Birthday parties Coffee mornings Discussion group in school Open Day Outings Over coffee after assemblies	Before or after formal meetings Bookstores Concerts and plays Home library Home-time chat Home visiting—pastoral or with program of work Parents helping in classroom Phone conversations	Discussion groups led by parents Anthologies of books recommended by parents Parents' rooms	Assemblies for parents Book fairs Evening talk Reading workshops	Booklets Vacation packs Letters and notices School magazine

Anthologies by Parents Parents who read to their children might be asked to review their favorite books and their children's. These could be made into a booklet available to all parents.

Arranged Visits An invitation might be given to a group of parents, or an individual, to visit the school and to look at the class with their child. The teacher may arrange that specific work on reading be going on, or chat with individual parents about reading in general.

Assemblies Prospective parents may be invited to an assembly or service during the course of which comments and advice about reading can be given. While they are in school, parents may be invited to observe their own children's class in action. Teachers can be present for a chat over coffee after assembly, when attention can be drawn to the various aspects of reading being used.

Birthday Parties Monthly parties for all children with a birthday during the month. Parents might organize the food and take part in games. The parties can provide informal setting for conversation.

Book Fairs It is important to give parents the opportunity to see a wide selection of children's books, and to have the chance to buy them. Inviting prospective parents along to a holiday or summer book fair is a useful introduction to the school.

Book Stores Some schools organize book stores and sell books to children. These book stores can be opened whenever parents and prospective parents are in school, and can offer for sale books for very young children. It is helpful if teachers can mingle with parents, to point out books which are known to be popular with any specific age group.

Booklets Booklets with advice to parents about preparing children for reading are helpful. They are best discussed with parents rather than simply sent out. They may also be displayed during evening talks, book fairs, and in the parents' room, and made available during open sessions and at preschool groups.

Class Teacher The class teacher has lots of opportunities to chat with parents in an informal way at school, but can also visit the home of all or some of the parents in her class. It is important that the first visit should be for a positive reason, for instance explaining the school's organization, but the topic of reading will arise in a natural way, and can then be a basis for discussion and advice.

Coffee Mornings After assembly coffee can be served to parents who have attended. These informal occasions can provide an opportunity for several kinds of contact. They are not places for lectures or formal talks, but those teachers who can be present have the chance to pick up any sensitive points, or to answer any question that parents may want to ask. Inviting prospective parents to coffee mornings run by present parents is very valuable.

Concerts and Plays Many parents will attend these occasions. If coffee is provided at some point there can be a good opportunity for discussion.

Discussion Group in Parents' Homes A meeting which occurs in the home of one parent, to which others have been invited. The parents of children who will soon be entering the school should not be forgotten. It helps if a teacher can be present at such a meeting.

Discussion Group in School At meetings arranged for groups of parents in school time, the principal, class teacher or an outside speaker can talk about particular topics. Schools which have organized babysitting have found that general relationships are helped if the visiting parents can talk without their younger children around.

Education Happening One-day exhibition of what's going on in school, usually held in park or shopping mall. Staff are available to meet parents and materials can be displayed.

Education Store Occasionally an empty store can be taken over for a few days. Preschool materials can be displayed and, whenever possible, staff should be available to answer parents' queries.

Evening Talk These can be arranged by the principal and staff, but they can also be requested by parents. Either the staff or an outside speaker may raise issues concerning reading and related matters. Programs should allow for the formal lecture, for small group talk, for informal chats, for looking at displays and materials, and for watching video and films.

Fixed Interviews These can be at the request of parent, principal or member of staff, at times of need. For example, with parents whose child will soon be starting school, teachers have found it valuable to spend time explaining what to expect, and how to make it easy for their son or daughter. At other times, teachers have invited parents in to discuss their child's progress, and parents have asked to talk about problems.

Home Library A selection of books which parents can borrow to read to their children. Some parents may welcome guidance on which books to choose. In some cases the library has been extended to include adult books, so that the child and parent can choose books together, and the parent is seen to be reading for pleasure and so acts as a model to the child.

Home Visiting Some schools have a teacher with home visiting as an explicit responsibility. Most teachers expect to be involved in home-school liaison, although one person may have the job of organizing or coordinating it all, and be allowed time for visits to discuss particular topics or issues. The teacher/coordinator, the class teacher and the principal can all be involved in the taking of materials, the discussion of particular problems, and the giving of advice.

Invitations It is extremely useful for parents and children to visit the classroom where the child is to become a student. Once the children have settled, it is possible for the principal to invite the parents for a cup of coffee to talk about the way the school will be working with their children. This can include a discussion of reading and the part parents can play.

Letters and Notices Letters can easily be formal and put parents off; and letters which apparently issue advice are not likely to be acted on. But letters to prospective parents can be important ways of establishing the relationship between school and home, and can introduce particular ideas to new parents. Teachers have found that it has been very useful to drop a note to parents about the good things their child has done ("Gary wrote a lovely story today about his grandmother") and to suggest ways of building on it ("Sally read *Frog and Toad Together* in the book corner today, and loved it. If you're looking for something to get for her birthday next week, she might like a copy of it. The Harper & Row book is inexpensive, and B. Dalton stocks it"). Finally, letters after events thanking parents for their participation and support are as important as the letters beforehand. The blackboard in the school playground is a simple way of presenting notices—"Thanks for everyone's support at the Summer Fair," as well as "There's a good after-school special on this week."

Newsletter Nursery schools and classes, or preschool groups can produce their own newsletter. This can be published yearly or half-yearly. Parents can help with articles, and with the typing, duplication and stapling. Copies can be distributed to all homes where there are children of preschool age.

Open School Day The formal, organized open school day is gradually being supplemented by informal contacts: many schools now have "open days" at regular times throughout the school year. Arranging occasionally for a day of activities concerning reading to coincide with the open school day, so that parents can see the value the school places on these activities, can be helpful. Such a day could include, for example, visits by a librarian to school, watching films, television, or listening to radio.

Open School Night Because the children are not there, there is the opportunity to concentrate on specific aspects of what the school is doing and has done. Literacy and literature can well form the basis of such an evening.

Outings Schools have arranged to take groups of parents and children to libraries or bookstores and exhibitions of books. These visits are mostly for parents of children already in school, but parents with children at nursery school or whose children will be coming during the next year, can be invited.

Parents Helping in School Parents have helped in two main ways: preparing materials in groups and helping in the classroom. The teacher can always organize it so that she is doing something about reading when the parents are there, and can then talk about it later over coffee. Equally, when a group is asked to prepare materials, the purpose of these materials can be explained.

Phone Conversations When parents telephone the school, they often have anxieties about their children. Apart from allaying their immediate anxieties, this can also be the opportunity to invite them in for some of the other contacts that are possible, and to discuss reading.

Play Group Teachers often have contact with local play groups, and so there is the opportunity for the school to pass on to parents of very young children some simple information about books, and hints about how the parents can help with their children's reading.

Preliminary Visits One kind of preliminary visit can be the evening talk to all parents of children who will be joining the school. More informally, groups of parents with their children can visit during school time and spend some time looking around. The principal can chat with the parents while their children have their first independent time in the class. During the visit, any necessary points about preparing their children for reading can be made.

Preschool Groups Some schools organize a group of parents and young children to meet regularly before the children start school. It can be a good idea for such a group to be based in the school and for a teacher to attend and help. Some schools have organized courses in preschool education for the parents who attend. The parents can also help in school: they provide extra adults to talk to the children and play prereading games.

Reading Workshop A series of sessions can be held either in or out of school time in which teachers discuss with the parents important factors in children learning to read. During each session specific suggestions are offered of ways in which parents can help their children, either at home or in the classroom.

Ready-for-School Meetings Either a single session or a series of sessions to advise parents on things they could do to make starting school easier for their child and to suggest preschool activities which could be done at home.

School Brochure Some school districts publish brochures and newsletters for parents of prospective pupils. These brochures can contain information about the school's approach to reading, and advice on how parents can support it. Some schools may consider that this kind of official brochure is not the place for such material, and may prefer to produce a less formal booklet to supply this information.

School Magazine Sending school magazines to prospective parents can help them to learn about the school and feel more a part of it. The magazines are particularly relevant when they include articles by parents and children, and possibly advice for parents.

Social Evening In some schools, parents arrange social activities to which teachers are invited. These are excellent opportunities to meet informally.

Trained Parents Parents who have attended a preschool group can disseminate ideas through visiting homes with preschool materials chosen by the teacher, or by leading discussion in another preschool group.

Vacation Packs A collection of educational activities and ideas for the children to do during school vacations. These can be distributed free, or sold cheaply to cover costs. A group of parents may be involved in duplication, collation and distribution.

Video/film Good videotapes or films of real situations involving reading are always more telling than lectures, and form an ideal basis for fruitful discussion. Many school districts now have facilities to enable a school to make its own videotapes. Education departments of colleges and universities in the area may be prepared to help.

3

A Prereading Program

The original idea of "prereading" was that there were ordinary but necessary activities that produced a willingness to read by providing experiences that generated interest. "Prereading," however, now seems to involve mainly, and sometimes exclusively, those matching, discriminating and sequencing activities widely marketed as "prereading activities."

There is no evidence which determines how valuable such activities are, although Margaret Clark in *Young Fluent Readers* does say that "great caution is needed in planning remediation programmes" based on apparent lack of visual discrimination. She adds, "it may be that the best way to improve . . . is to practise reading."

Experienced teachers, unable to agree on the value of visual discrimination exercises, defined the following as the environment which would be most likely to encourage the desire to read, that is, the best "prereading program."

an inviting classroom, with a comfy area, and an inviting book corner.

security for the children in a relaxed, unthreatening atmosphere.

lots of beautiful books and the experience of handling them.

the experience of seeing, as well as hearing, the teacher read.

written language in sentences around the room, not isolated words (unless the words are in particular contexts, e.g., "Boys" on the lavatory door).

labels on displays, made by both children and teacher.

creation of an environment in which communication is real—sending notes and getting answers to them, mailing letters, inviting other classes in for activities, by letter or card.

hearing stories at different times of the day.

watching TV, listening to taped stories.

dressing up, playing in the play house, playing with puppets.

playing games like chutes and ladders, dominoes, jigsaws.

encouraging children to notice what is different about the classroom from day to day.

A "prereading program" which creates this classroom environment should be experienced by all children as a matter of course.

Visual Perception

Much has been written about the advisability of providing specific training in visual perception as part of the pre-reading programme. The evidence is inconclusive, but on balance such training seems only to be of value for children who have had a rather limited range of perceptual experience. Once a child has achieved a degree of proficiency* there seems to be little gain in spending time on general perceptual learning.

A Language for Life: The Bullock Report (7.9)

The whole area of "visual perception as part of the prereading programme" is contentious. The points agreed upon by experienced teachers are:

If a child is proficient in the normal kindergarten class activities, visual perception tests are almost certainly unnecessary.

"Perceptual experience" is naturally acquired by children before they come to school as they help with setting the table, doing dishes, housework and jobs around the house.

If children have not had the normal routines of domestic experience, what they have missed may form the basis of discussion with parents, who are always anxious to help their children, and may not have recognized the importance of these ordinary experiences. For the school, these, or concentrated activities like them, should become the staple diet of the kindergarten class.

If the children can cope with the ordinary activities in the kindergarten class like singing, playing, painting, drawing and copying, then they have the necessary "degree of proficiency." If they can't cope it is these things they need to practice, not specially produced visual or auditory discrimination tasks.

Where it is felt that children must be given some kinds of matching, sequencing and discriminating experience, the activities should go alongside the normal ones that precede reading. They should be done with words in meaningful sentences, not with jigsaws, patterns and shapes. Jigsaws have their place but for different purposes, which may not have any effect on a child's perceptions of written language.

*"Degree of proficiency" is normally assumed to cover what one expects an ordinary five-year-old to be able to do.

In her study *Young Fluent Readers* Margaret Clark writes:

> Almost without exception, children have the visual perception and the auditory discrimination adequate for learning to read.

Writing about the specific tests she applied in her study, she comments that of her group of children, all of whom were able to read before they went to school, "few of these children were above average in tasks involving visual discrimination" (Clark, 1976).

Specific Visual Problems

The question of acuity is more specialized, but the following points may be made.

Normal vision means being able to look at things and see them the way they are. Assume that children can do this unless you see evidence that they can't, for example:

narrowing or widening the eyes.

leaning forward to look at something.

holding something close or further away to look at it.

inability to see something at a distance.

squinting or rubbing eyes a lot.

"lazy" eyes.

avoiding close work.

holding book to one side instead of in front of the face.

If a child does any of these things, arrange for eye tests.

Children may not know how to handle books, and may hold them the wrong way up, or begin at the wrong end. This is not evidence of visual or perceptual weaknesses. Programs of prereading activities such as visual discrimination activities and matching cards are less valuable to such children than the experience of handling books, being read to, and sharing the stories and pictures with an adult. For a discussion of reading aloud and a list of books for that purpose, refer to *Literature and the Child* by Cullinan, Karrer, and Pillar (Harcourt, 1981), pp. 454–56 and 502–503.

Some wordless books children can "read" independently are:

Briggs, Raymond *The Snowman* Random House, 1978

Carle, Eric *Catch the Ball* Philomel, 1982
    Let's Paint a Rainbow Philomel, 1982

dePaola, Tomie *Pancakes for Breakfast* Harcourt Brace Jovanovich, 1978

Goodall, John S. *Shrewbettina's Birthday* Voyager, 1983
Jacko Voyager, 1984

Krahn, Fernando *Arthur's Adventures in the Abandoned House* Dutton, 1981

Lionni, Leo *When?* Pantheon, 1983
Who? Pantheon, 1983
Where? Pantheon, 1983
What? Pantheon, 1983

Massie, Diane *Cocoon* Crowell, 1983

Morris, Terry Nell *Good Night, Dear Monster!* Knopf, 1980

Turkle, Brinton *Deep in the Forest* Dutton, 1976

Young, Ed *Up a Tree* Harper, 1983

Help for Specific Problems

If children seem to have no idea what books are or what they are for: Give them plenty of experience of having stories told to them, being read to, handling books themselves, following taped stories, or (if slides are available) having the pictures projected as the story is told.

If you suspect a child has visual problems: Contact the school nurse.

If you suspect a child has hearing loss or problems: Contact the school nurse.

Finally, a child's medical history, especially if there was a difficult birth, or a serious illness like meningitis or scarlet fever, may suggest potential problems; such problems may not be "perceptual" but neurological in origin.

4

Organizing a Reading Program

The *reading program* is the total set of activities and materials a school uses to teach reading. A *reading series* is one published set of graded readers. In the past, a school's total reading program was often a single published reading series. Increasingly, the reading program uses the series as only one part of the materials for teaching reading. Sometimes, all children are expected to encounter certain materials in the course of learning to read. This represents the *core* of the reading program.

Usually the core is one of these:

a published reading series.

a mixture of different published reading series.

a program with central materials such as *Breakthrough to Literacy*.

a wide selection of trade books.

Using Reading Series as Part of the Reading Programs

Four methods of organization are described. The first is closest to the conventional reading series, the third and fourth are nearest to free-choice reading.

An important consequence of learning to read ought to be that a child wants to read, and knows how to make choices. Children can only learn to choose if a suitable range of materials is available to choose from. This is not necessarily to suggest totally free choice: children should be encouraged to choose from a range that the teacher has previously selected. A teacher, however, is able to select on the grounds of a reading level, but can't necessarily predict what will be of interest. Children will cope with texts apparently too difficult, if the topic is important to them.

Method One: Supplementing the Series

The reading series is supplemented with books from other reading series. The child may be allowed to choose from books of a similar level. Information about comparable books in a variety of basal series is available from individual publishers. The International Reading Association (800 Barksdale Road, Newark, Delaware 19714) has extensive publications to assist teachers.

Method Two: Supplementing the Series with "Real" Books

The reading series is supplemented with real books—trade books, etc. When children have completed the appropriate book on the reading series, they are allowed free choice of the books which have been selected as being of a similar level of difficulty.

If the children get stuck on the reading series book, they are encouraged to turn to other books on that shelf, returning to the reading series when they are more confident and competent.

Publishers' catalogues are invaluable aids for book selection. They are organized both according to subject/interest and to level of difficulty. In addition, the many fine textbooks on children's literature (e.g., *Literature and the Child* by Cullinan, Karrer, and Pillar) provide detailed descriptions of trade books to supplement basal series. Scholastic Book Services, Inc. (50 West 44th Street, New York, New York 10036) publishes *Text Extenders* for the same purpose.

Method Three: Shelving by Levels

Books are arranged by shelves according to their level of difficulty. The books are predominantly trade books, with reading series books included where appropriate.

The children are allowed free choice within the range. The reading series book may be regarded as essential at some time, although some teachers may be prepared to allow children who are making obvious progress to skip basal series books.

The intention is to offer the children an extensive selection of reading, yet at the same time to avoid the sense of failure which children may have if they try to cope with books that are too difficult.

Here, for instance, are examples from one school's organization of books into levels. The levels are in half-years—5.0–5.5, 5.5–6.0 and so on. Two levels only are illustrated here.

Reading Age 5.5–6.0

Single Books

Anno, Mitsumasa *Anno's Counting House* Philomel, 1982

Brown, Marc *Arthur's Thanksgiving* Little, Brown, 1983

Cooney, Barbara *Miss Rumphius* Viking, 1982

Duke, Kate *The Guinea Pig ABC* Dutton, 1983

Isadora, Rachel *City Seen from A to Z* Greenwillow, 1983

Louis, Ai-Ling *Yeh-Shen: A Cinderella Story from China*
Philomel, 1982

Marshall, James *George and Martha Back in Town* Houghton
Mifflin, 1984

Stanley, Diane *The Conversation Club* Macmillan, 1983

Sets of Books

Harcourt Brace Jovanovich:

Look, Listen, and Learn
Sounds, Symbols, and Sense
Sun Up
Happy Morning
Magic Afternoon
Sun and Shadow
Together We Go

Macmillan:

Starting Out
Make Your Mark
Off We Go
You Can
I Can, Too
We Can Read
Opening Doors
Rainbow World

Scott, Foresman:

Away We Go
Taking Off
Going Up
On Our Way
Hang On To Your Hats
Keep Up Your Heels

Ginn:

One Potato, Two
Little Dog Laughed
Fish and Not Fish
Inside My Hat
Birds Fly, Bears Don't
Across the Fence

Reading Age 7.0–7.5

Single Books

Alexander, Sue *Nadia the Willful* Pantheon, 1983

Fleischman, Paul *Graven Images* Harper & Row, 1982

Fritz, Jean *Homesick: My Own Story* Putnam, 1982

Hoban, Lillian *Arthur's Funny Money* Harper & Row, 1983

Hopkins, Lee Bennett *The Sky Is Full of Song* Harper &
Row, 1983

Kennedy, X. J. and Dorothy M.   *Knock at a Star: A Child's Introduction to Poetry*   Little, Brown, 1982

Seuss, Dr.   *The Butter Battle Book*   Random House, 1984

Speare, Elizabeth George   *The Sign of the Beaver*   Houghton Mifflin, 1983

Sets of Books

Harcourt Brace Jovanovich:

World of Surprises
People and Places

Macmillan:

Magic Times
Mirrors and Images

Scott, Foresman:

Rainbow Shower
Crystal Kingdom

Ginn:

Glad to Meet You
Give Me a Clue

Method Four: Shelving by Theme or Topic

A reading level is indicated inside the back cover of each book. The books can then be shelved alphabetically, or by theme, or in any other order which is like the organization of real libraries. The children can choose from any shelf.

This method allows children to read any book for pleasure, rather than having the stigma of being confined to any one book, level or shelf. The teacher can monitor the kind of choice the children make, and can observe the level of the books each child chooses.

Deciding on Levels

Making decisions about assigning books to levels is a job for the entire teaching staff. The discussion involved in determining the coding for books will help staff become familiar with them. We suggest using only broad grouping because it gets very complicated otherwise.

There are two disadvantages in making ability levels public. First, less confident readers may feel held back. Secondly, able readers may feel that they shouldn't take a simpler book which they would like to read, because those books are for lower-level readers.

The following are general guidelines available for helping staff to decide on levels:

Publishers' suggestions, but these are often arbitrary.

Trade advice from public libraries, and children's librarians; library leaflets recommend books, but do not often indicate age-ranges.

Use magazines and reviews to inform discussion: for instance, *The*

Horn Book, School Library Journal, Bulletin of the Center for Children's Books (the University of Chicago Press), *Literature and the Child* (textbook from Harcourt Brace Jovanovich)

A checklist for the evaluation of reading programs by Sidney Rauch appears in *The Reading Teacher* (March, 1968, pp. 519–22).

For combining series and trade books an excellent guide is *Text Extenders* from Scholastic Book Services, Inc. Also see Teacher's Editions from the basal's publishers.

Finally, there is no substitute for a staff deciding on its own criteria, and applying them to books in school.

Resources to Supplement Core Materials

Once a school has chosen a method of organization, decisions will need to be made about which materials to use. Some examples are suggested here.

Books

Fiction

picture books.

stories for younger children.

junior fiction in general: for young children, a selection of suitable junior fiction can be made available.

The current publishers' catalogues and backlists are most reliable sources for selecting books for each of these categories. Where possible, a visit to the Children's Book Council (67 Irving Place, New York, New York 10003) is essential. The Council houses all books for children published within the most recent 3-year period.

Nonfiction

The choice of nonfiction is complex. Basically, care should be taken not to limit too much the *kinds* of reading pupils may wish to do. The staff might discuss what topics are to be represented, and then order books about the topic which range from the simplest to the more complex. When there is such a range, it allows pupils to go to the book which best caters for what they want, rather than having to begin with the simple "starter" books. Children may know a good deal about something even if they are not very good at reading.

For example, assume that the staff has decided that *Computers* and *Dinosaurs* are two suitable topics. The range of books provided might look like this:

Books about computers

Ault, Rosalie Sain *Basic Programming for Kids* Houghton Mifflin, 1984

Bartholomew, Barbara (Yuri Salzman, illus.) *The Great Grade-point Mystery* Macmillan, 1983

Berger, Melvin *Computers in Your Life* Harper & Row, 1984

Bly, Robert W. *Computers: PASCAL, Pong and Pac-Man* Banbury, 1984

D'Ignazio, Fred *Chip Mitchell: The Case of the Stolen Computer Brains* Lodestar, 1983

Jespersen, James and Jane Fitz-Randolph *Rams, Roms, & Robots: The Inside Story of Computers* Atheneum, 1984

Lipson, Shelley (Janice Stapleton, illus.) *It's BASIC* Holt, Rinehart & Winston, 1984

Lord, Harvey G. *Programming for Real* Atheneum, 1984

Markle, Sandra (Stella Ormai, illus.) *The Programmer's Guide to the Galaxy* Lothrop, 1984

Math, Irwin *Bits and Pieces: Understanding and Building Computing Devices* Scribner, 1984

McMahan, Ian (Yuri Salzman, illus.) *The Fox's Lair* Macmillan, 1983

Mitchell, Joyce S. *Your Job in the Computer Age: The Computer Skills You Will Need to Get the Job You Want* Scribner, 1984

Simon, Seymour (Steven Lindblom, illus.) *Computer Sense, Computer Nonsense* Lippincott, 1984

Sullivan, George *Computer Kids* Dodd, Mead 1984

Books about dinosaurs

Bates, Robin and Cheryl Simon (Jennifer Dewey, illus.) *The Dinosaurs and the Mystery Star* Macmillan, 1984

Brown, Marc and Stephen Krensky *Dinosaurs, Beware! A Safety Guide* Atlantic, 1982

Cohen, Daniel *Monster Dinosaur* Lippincott, 1983

Elting, Mary (John Hamberger, illus.) *The Macmillan Book of Dinosaurs & Other Prehistoric Creatures* Macmillan, 1984

Emberley, Michael *Dinosaurs! A Drawing Book* Little, Brown, 1980

Freedman, Russell (Leslie Morrill, illus.) *Dinosaurs and Their Young* Holiday, 1983

Mannetti, William *Dinosaurs in Your Backyard* Atheneum, 1982

Moseley, Keith (Robert Cremins, illus.) *Dinosaurs: A Lost World* Putnam, 1984

Most, Bernard *If The Dinosaurs Came Back* Harcourt Brace Jovanovich, 1984

Sattler, Helen Roney (Jean Day Zallinger, illus.) *Baby Dinosaurs* Lothrop, 1984

Sattler, Helen (Anthony Rao, illus.) *Dinosaurs of North America* Lothrop, 1981

The books can be shelved together by theme, with their "level" marked inside the cover.

It is not always easy to know a suitable range of books for topics. Ways to find out are:

consult pupils about good books they have read on topics they are interested in.

ask pupils to consult their parents, especially if the parent has a known expertise.

ask local librarians.

consult school librarians.

consult experts, appropriate societies and associations: write letters asking for help and advice.

The need to offer children a complete range of books would seem to indicate the value of housing nonfiction books centrally.

Other Reading Material

What is available dictates what will be chosen for reading, and a wide range of available material introduces the idea of reading for different purposes, so it is important to provide other printed reading materials. A range chosen from the following materials should be in every primary classroom.

picture books without words.

books that are nicely illustrated but too difficult for children to read on their own.

reference books, about the exotic (dinosaurs) but also about things familiar but unnoticed—buses, toys, fish.

dictionaries, encyclopedias, thesauruses.

maps, atlases, road maps.

puzzle and quiz books.

TV Guide, local PBS program guides, newspapers.

magazines.

football programs.

comics.

directories, mail-order catalogues.

instructions, manuals.

sports schedules and results (local team and school).

school lunch menus.

timetables—school, train, bus.

notices, posters for current events, ads.

labels (relevant ones).

birthday cards, invitations.

labelled photographs, picture postcards.

contests—leaflets, magazines, cereal boxes.

material written by other children (in and out of school).

Children's Own Writing

What children have written has been used by some schools as a valuable resource for reading. Below are examples of actual practice from elementary schools:

stories written by children in the same class for each other.

stories written by older children for younger children.

class and school magazines.

photograph albums of school visits, captioned by pupils.

children's utterances, written down by teacher, or by themselves.

collections of writing (e.g., autobiographies, vacation stories) with contents and indexes.

Children find each other's handwriting hard to read, and if it is possible their work should be typed and "published." Printing it in this way makes it public property, and the process gives the teacher, or older pupils, the opportunity to proofread the work and so to give help with spelling, punctuation and so on.

Children's writing is influenced by what they read, which gives them "models" to draw on. If they have read only basal readers, their writing will sound like the language of basals. Through their reading they need to experience as wide a range as possible of kinds of writing.

Audio-Visual Materials

Books can be read onto tape, and the book and tape made available. This can be done with a selection of the books that are in the classroom, or in the school's general collection. The tape encourages the children to follow the text while they listen. Use either a cassette playback or a listening center (a set of earphones attached through a junction box to a cassette recorder or playback). Once they have heard a story and followed it in the text, many children want to read the book to themselves, without the support of the tape.

A useful machine is "Language Master" made by Bell & Howell. A card with a strip of recording-tape is fed through the machine and the teacher records whatever is desired—a reading of the text written on the card, questions, comments, or instructions. The tape has two tracks, so pupils can record their own versions. When the card is fed through the machine the voice is played back, and the pupil can simultaneously read whatever is written on the card. Language Masters can be used for:

talking dictionaries.

audio games connected with reading.

Slide strips are available to show the pictures of a book while the text is being read. If this is done, children can add their own commentary to the pictures. Tape-slide presentations are also available, in which a commercially produced tape presents a reading to go alongside slides of the illustrations. Animated films are produced by Weston Woods, and some public libraries have them available on loan.

5

Choosing Books for Children and Helping Them to Choose for Themselves

> It's no good telling children that the books they love to read are no good; because you're actually saying to the child, "You're no good for choosing these no good books." You must look for what's satisfying to them in these books; and, if you're any good, you know another book that will help them enjoy something more subtle.
>
> Margaret Meek

When selecting books for children the following three points are important:

1. Content: topic and language.

2. Attractiveness: visual and handling appeal.

3. Ease of reading: including difficulty and legibility of text.

1 Content

Story

Teachers and researchers all recognize the powerful need young children have for story. Even if children are too young to read alone, they still respond to stories told or read; reading them stories which they can't yet read themselves is an important way of leading children into an understanding of what books are for.

Most of the traditional fare for the young is story—folktales, fairy tales, and cumulative tales (e.g., "The House That Jack Built" and "The Gingerbread Man"). Some research (e.g., Whitehead, Spencer) suggests that unless children have been offered a substantial diet of storybooks, they will be unlikely to become readers. Because they have never experienced the pleasure of stories, they see little point in reading at all.

Relevance

The idea of "relevance" can be interpreted too simply to mean that an inner-city child should only be shown books with inner-city scenes, and a rural child should only see books about the country. A more helpful way of considering relevance is to ask: Do children *recognize* in the book any aspects of their own everyday life, or their inner world of imagination and fantasy? The answer to the question will depend on how far the story captures one of the inevitable experiences of growing-up. For instance, all young children feel at some stage a fear that they will be abandoned or lost by their parents, so they enjoy the sensations of fear and relief in safety, by meeting relevant stories.

Books about being lost and abandoned

For younger children

Barton, Byron *Where's Al* Houghton Mifflin, 1972

Bemelmans, Ludwig *Madeline & the Gypsies* Penguin, 1977

Cohen, Miriam *Lost in the Museum* Greenwillow, 1979

Goble, Paul & Dorothy *Friendly Wolf* Bradbury, 1975

Haley, Gail E. *The Green Man* Scribner, 1980

Jeffers, Susan *Hansel & Gretel* Dial, 1980

McCloskey, Robert *Blueberries for Sal* Penguin, 1976

For older children

Bunting, Eve *If I Asked You, Would You Stay?* Lippincott, 1984

Byars, Betsy *The Two-Thousand Pound Goldfish* Harper & Row, 1982

Cameron, Eleanor *The Court of the Stone Children* Dutton, 1973

Klein, Norma *Bizou* Viking, 1983

Phipson, Joan *A Tide Flowing* Atheneum, 1981

Voigt, Cynthia *Homecoming* Atheneum, 1981

Walsh, Jill Paton *A Chance Child* Farrar, Straus and Giroux, 1978

Similarly, because all children find a great many things frightening—the dark, closed rooms, monsters, noises at night, and so on—they welcome books which deal with such fears, especially if they deal with them humorously. There is a whole range of these psychological needs, and one important definition of *relevance* is that books should provide a safe framework in which to explore some of the troubling, distressing or frightening experiences and feelings which are inevitable for everyone.

Books about fear and terror

Berenstain, Stanley & Janice   *Bears in the Night*   Random House, 1971

Bonsall, Crosby   *Who's Afraid of the Dark?*   Harper & Row, 1980

Chambers, Aidan   *The Present Takers*   Harper & Row, 1984

Dragonwagon, Crescent   *Will It Be Okay?*   Harper & Row, 1977

Eisenberg, Phyllis Rose   *Don't Tell Me a Ghost Story*   Harcourt Brace Jovanovich, 1982

Francis, Anna B.   *Pleasant Dreams*   Holt, Rinehart & Winston, 1983

Gackenbach, Dick   *Harry & the Terrible Whatzit*   Clarion, 1984

Hoban, Russell   *Bedtime for Frances*   Harper & Row, 1976

Knowles, Anne   *The Halcyon Island*   Harper & Row, 1981

Orlev, Uri   *The Island on Bird Street*   Houghton Mifflin, 1984

Potter, Beatrix   *The Tale of Mister Tod*   Warne, 1912

Reed, Jonathan   *Do Armadillos Come in Houses?*   Atheneum, 1981

Sharmat, Marjorie Weinman   *Frizzy the Fearful*   Holiday, 1983

Stevenson, James   *What's Under My Bed?*   Greenwillow, 1983

Stren, Patti   *I'm Only Afraid of the Dark (at Night!!)*   Harper & Row, 1982

Stubbs, Joanna   *With Cat's Eyes You'll Never Be Afraid of the Dark*   Deutsch, 1983

Another equally important but less dramatic kind of relevance is that which shows a child the fuller meaning of everyday experiences, presenting them in such a way that readers can begin to value their own everyday life, and see the importance of what is normally taken for granted. Finally, relevance has to do with coming to terms with other people, and empathizing with them in ways that illuminate one's own life.

Books about everyday experiences

Estes, Eleanor   *The Hundred Dresses*   Harcourt Brace, 1944

Hest, Amy   *The Crack-of-Dawn Walkers*   Macmillan, 1984

Hoban, Tana *Round & Round & Round* Greenwillow, 1983

Hoopes, Lyn Littlefield *When I Was Little* Unicorn, 1983

Kherdian, David & Nonny Hogrogian *Right Now* Knopf, 1983

Zalben, Jane Breskin *Oliver and Alison's Week* Farrar, Straus and Giroux, 1980

For older readers

Beckman, Delores *My Own Private Sky* Dutton, 1980

Byars, Betsy *The Night Swimmers* Delacorte, 1980

Cleary, Beverly *Dear Mr. Henshaw* Morrow, 1983

Hunter, Mollie *Hold on to Love* Harper & Row, 1984

Nostlinger, Christine *Marrying Off Mother* Harcourt Brace Jovanovich, 1982

Oneal, Zibby *A Formal Feeling* Viking, 1982

It is important to be aware of possible bias and stereotyping. Social class bias is now something most people are conscious of, and teachers tend to avoid books where children always dress immaculately, play in enormous gardens, and never quarrel or look unhappy, dirty or hungry. Less obvious is racial bias: obvious kinds can be picked out, but there are less obvious kinds too, like the absence of multi-ethnic characters.

Books without racial bias

Appiah, Peggy *Tales of an Ashanti Father* Deutsch, 1981

Caines, Jeannette *Abby* Harper Trophy, 1984

Clifton, Lucille *Everett Anderson's Goodbye* Holt, Rinehart & Winston, 1983

Hamilton, Virginia *The Magical Adventures of Pretty Pearl* Harper & Row, 1983

Hurmence, Belinda *Tancy* Clarion, 1984

Myers, Walter Dean *Hoops* Delacorte, 1981

Wilkinson, Brenda *Ludell's New York Time* Harper & Row, 1980

Sex-role bias is also present in some books. Teachers are becoming more aware of the books, sometimes of high literary merit, which still present children and adults in stereotyped activities, divided into masculine and feminine worlds, often at the expense of the female. Some books rarely mention girls or women, others use "negative" female characters, presented as silly or unthinking.

Several lists of nonsexist reading books have been published, but some of the books recommended do not remove the stereotypes. The characters are still traditionally stereotyped, but the sexes are reversed. Teachers should be wary of using these, because they present another, equally unhelpful kind of stereotyping.

Books with positive female characters

Alexander, Lloyd   *The Beggar Queen*   Dutton, 1984

Caines, Jeannette   *Just Us Women*   Harper & Row, 1982

Cleaver, Vera & Bill   *Hazel Rye*   Lippincott, 1983

Cooney, Ellen   *Small-Town Girl*   Houghton Mifflin, 1983

dePaola, Tomie   *Helga's Dowry*   Harcourt Brace Jovanovich, 1977
        Fin M'Coul: The Giant of Knockmany Hill
        Holiday, 1981

Greene, Bette   *Them That Glitter & Them That Don't*   Knopf, 1983

Hague, Kathleen & Michael   *The Man Who Kept House*
    Harcourt Brace Jovanovich, 1981

Lindgren, Astrid   *Roma, the Robber's Daughter*   Viking, 1983

Rabe, Berniece   *The Balancing Girl*   Dutton, 1981

Vinke, Hermann   *The Short Life of Sophie Scholl*   Harper & Row, 1984

Voigt, Cynthia   *Dicey's Song*   Atheneum, 1982

Walsh, Jill Paton   *A Parcel of Patterns*   Farrar, Straus and Giroux, 1983

Yep, Laurence   *The Serpent's Children*   Harper & Row, 1984

To summarize the idea of relevant content:

it should offer images relating to the inner and outer life of children.

it should help children to deal in safety with inevitable worries and fears.

it should present everyday life in a recognizable and meaningful way.

it should encourage understanding of one's own and other people's lives and problems.

Humor

Children respond enthusiastically to funny books and stories, and humor in a book is a great encouragement to them to want to read it. Not all of the things that children find funny will amuse adults: and what adults find funny, children will often take quite seriously. Different aged children like different kinds of jokes.

Humorous books
For younger children

Brown, Marc   *What Do You Call a Dumb Bunny?*   Atlantic, 1983

dePaola, Tomie   *The Mysterious Giant of Barletta*   Harcourt Brace Jovanovich, 1984

Fleischman, Paul   *Finzel the Farsighted*   Dutton, 1983

Kellogg, Steven   *Ralph's Secret Weapon*   Dial, 1983

Wiseman, Bernard   *Doctor Duck & Nurse Swan*   Dutton, 1984

For older children

Danziger, Paula   *There's a Bat in Bunk Five*   Delacorte, 1980

Howe, James   *Howliday Inn*   Atheneum, 1982

King-Smith, Dick   *Magnus Powermouse*   Harper & Row, 1984

Lowry, Lois   *Anastasia, Ask Your Analyst*   Houghton Mifflin, 1984

Raskin, Ellen   *The Westing Game*   Dutton, 1980

Characters

Certain characters in stories are always popular. Animals are favorites because any child, whatever age, sex, color or shape, can identify with an animal. Kings, queens, princes, princesses, wizards, witches, and other folktale characters are constantly popular.

But this is a complex area: spiders, caterpillars and ogres don't seem attractive, but can be well-liked. "Characters" seem, in fact, less important than "relevance": if the child recognizes the story, as suggested above, it won't matter who or what it's about.

Animal characters
For younger children

Galdone, Paul   *The Three Little Pigs*   Clarion, 1984

Godden, Rumer   *The Mousewife*   Viking, 1982

McPhail, David   *Pig Pig Goes to Camp*   Dutton, 1983

Muntean, Michaela & Nicole Rubel   *The House That Bear Built*   Dial, 1984

Sharmat, Marjorie Weinman   *Bartholomew the Bossy*   Macmillan, 1984

Steig, William   *Doctor De Soto*   Farrar, Straus and Giroux, 1982

Thaler, Mike   *It's Me, Hippo*   Harper & Row, 1983

Wildsmith, Brian   *Daisy*   Pantheon, 1984

For older children

Bell, Clare   *Ratha's Creature*   Atheneum, 1983

Corbett, W. J.   *The Song of Pentecost*   Dutton, 1983

Cunningham, Julia   *Wolf Roland*   Pantheon, 1983

Graham, Kenneth   *The Wind in the Willows*   Viking, 1983

Howe, James & Deborah   *Bunnicula: A Rabbit Tale of Mystery*   Atheneum, 1979

Hurd, Edith Thacher   *Song of the Sea Otter*   Sierra Club/ Pantheon, 1983

King-Smith, Dick   *Pigs Might Fly*   Viking, 1982

Wangerin, Walter Jr.   *The Book of the Dun Cow*   Harper & Row, 1978

2   Attractiveness

Illustrations

Pictures are important because they often tell the story or part of it. They are an enormous potential aid to the full reading of text. Pictures offer clues to the meaning of text; they extend the text; sometimes they subtly contradict the text.

Rosie's Walk has a deadpan text of only 32 words—"Rosie the hen went for a walk . . . past the mill . . . under the beehives . . ."—which is silent about the disasters occurring to the fox who is hunting Rosie, who remains as unconscious of her pursuer as the text is. This is an example of a book where the text and the picture are both necessary: either of them on its own gives only half the story. Text and picture are totally inter-related, so that neither can stand without the other.

The question of what *kind* of picture is not one that can be answered by formula. Sometimes, children who are starting to read respond to clear bright illustrations that are simple and obvious. Tomie dePaola's illustrations and books are generally popular, because of their vitality and wit, as are Leo and Diane Dillon's books. The work of complex illustrators like Brian Wildsmith and David Macaulay should be available too.

Two other aspects of pictures shouldn't be omitted. Irrespective of their quality, highly detailed pictures fascinate children, who will explore both the familiar and the exotic. And a picture can be a talking point, both for the children themselves, and for the teacher and children together.

Handling Appeal

Although they are more expensive than paperbacks, some beautiful hardbound books should be made available, kept on accessible shelves so that they can be handled by the children.

The paper used for children's books is excellent on the whole; but the publications of book clubs that use cheap paper and stapled bindings should be avoided.

A selection of appealing children's books

Baskin, Leonard *Hosie's Zoo* Viking, 1981

Carle, Eric *The Secret Birthday Message* Crowell, 1972

Cauley, Lorinda Bryan *The Goose and the Golden Coins* Harcourt Brace Jovanovich, 1981

Gerrard, Roy & Jean *Matilda Jane* Farrar, Straus and Giroux, 1983

Gibbons, Gail *Sun Up, Sun Down* Harcourt Brace Jovanovich, 1983

Graham, Lorenz *Song of the Boat* Crowell, 1975

Jeffers, Susan, illus. *Hansel & Gretel* Dial, 1980

Kellogg, Steven *Ralph's Secret Weapon* Dial, 1983

Lobel, Arnold *Fables* Harper & Row, 1980

Mayer, Mercer *The Sleeping Beauty* Macmillan, 1984

Macaulay, David *Castle* Houghton Mifflin, 1977

Van Allsburg, Chris *Ben's Dream* Houghton Mifflin, 1982

Wells, Rosemary *Peabody* Dial, 1983

Wildsmith, Brian *Daisy* Pantheon, 1984

Zolotow, Charlotte *If You Listen* Harper & Row, 1980

3   Ease of Reading

Language

For the very young child certain kinds of reading material must present a problem. Such sequences as "look, look, see the elephant" do not come naturally off the tongue of the average five-year-old in everyday speech. Reading material which presents children with this unreal language therefore lacks predictability and prevents them from making use of the sequential probability in linguistic structure. The result is that they have to depend too much on a laboured phonic approach to unfamiliar words.

A Language for Life: The Bullock Report (6.34)

There is considerable controversy over "structured" versus "unstructured" texts, and these notes will not attempt to resolve the argument. There is, though, general agreement that written language which is "natural," that is, similar to the rhythms and structures of natural spoken language, encourages reading more than does stilted and contrived repetitive language.

Because of this, reading materials ought to include stories and books written by the children themselves. As Donald Graves suggests, child-made books must be treated as literature. These can be made by teachers from the sentences written by children, or from the children's talking and writing about their interests, expressed in their own language. Because they are close to their natural rhythms of talk such books are read with ease, and enable the children to see themselves as writers and authors from an early age. Repetition, where it is natural, is important, and many well-loved stories have refrains which recur and are added to.

Stories with repetition and refrains

Aardema, Verna *Bringing the Rain to Kapiti Plain* Dial, 1981

Gag, Wanda *Millions of Cats* Putnam, 1928

Galdone, Paul *Gingerbread Boy* Clarion, 1983
Henny Penny Scholastic, 1980
Three Billy Goats Gruff Clarion, 1981

Hoberman, Mary Ann *A House Is a House for Me* Viking, 1982

Hoguet, Susan Ramsay *I Unpacked My Grandmother's Trunk* Dutton, 1983

Martin, Bill Jr. *Brown Bear, Brown Bear, What Do You See?* Holt, Rinehart & Winston, 1983

It is hard to predict what will cause difficulties. Many stories which may be felt to be too hard do not cause the difficulties expected: some of the Beatrix Potter books are examples of this, and so are the pop-up and game books. What seems to happen is that children take from the story what they wish, and do not bother about the "difficulties."

Beginning books

Chalmers, Mary   *Take a Nap, Harry*   Harper Trophy, 1981
Merry Christmas   Harper Trophy, 1981
Be Good, Harry   Harper Trophy, 1981
Throw a Kiss, Harry   Harper Trophy, 1981

Chorao, Kay   *Kate's Car*   Dutton, 1982
Kate's Box   Dutton, 1982
Kate's Quilt   Dutton, 1982
Kate's Snowman   Dutton, 1982

Ginsburg, Mirra   *Good Morning, Chick*   Greenwillow, 1980

Gundersheimer, Karen   *1 2 3 Play With Me*   Harper & Row, 1984
A B C Say With Me   Harper & Row, 1984

Hague, Michael   *Mother Goose*   Holt Rinehart & Winston, 1984

Hoban, Russell   *Jim Frog*   Holt Rinehart & Winston, 1984
Big John Turkle   Holt, Rinehart & Winston, 1984

Johnson, Crockett   *Harold and the Purple Crayon*   Harper & Row, 1955
Harold's Trip to the Sky   Harper & Row, 1957
Harold's Circus   Harper & Row, 1959
Harold's ABC   Harper & Row, 1963

Kitchen, Bert   *Animal Alphabet*   Dial, 1984

Kozikowski, Renate   *Titus Bear Goes to Bed*   Harper & Row, 1984
Titus Bear Goes to School   Harper & Row, 1984
Titus Bear Goes to the Beach   Harper & Row, 1984

McNaughton, Colin   *Summer*   Dial, 1984
Spring   Dial, 1984
Winter   Dial, 1984
Autumn   Dial, 1984

Oxenbury, Helen   *The First Day of School*   Dial, 1983
The Car Trip   Dial, 1983
The Checkup   Dial, 1983

Peppe, Rodney   *Little Wheels*   Viking, 1983
Little Games   Viking, 1983
Little Numbers   Viking, 1983
Little Dolls   Viking, 1983
Little Circus   Viking, 1983

Rockwell, Anne & Harlow   *My Back Yard*   Macmillan, 1984
When I Go Visiting   Macmillan, 1984

Schroeder, Binette   *Tuffa and the Bone*   Dial, 1983
Tuffa and the Ducks   Dial, 1983
Tuffa and Her Friends   Dial, 1983
Tuffa and the Snow   Dial, 1983
Tuffa and the Picnic   Dial, 1983

Seymour, Peter   *Turn and Learn Books*   Macmillan, 1984

Legibility

For very young children, the print should not pose unnecessary problems. The following points can be noted:

Lower case bold print is the easiest to read. Italic is difficult. Capital letters *may* cause difficulties.

An ideal line of type contains not more than twelve words, and may be shorter in the earliest stages: but the number of words is less important than the spaced covered. A line shouldn't stretch for more than six to seven inches at most: if it's longer, it's hard to read.

Size

There should be books of all sizes available, from the pocket-sized books of Beatrix Potter through to the large-format book, both "portrait" and "landscape" in design.

Browsing

Having insured that a wide variety of reading materials of all kinds is available and accessible, you will need to help children to learn how to make choices.

Browsing is an important thing to learn, and many children will need to be taught how to do it. It should not be taught necessarily as a class lesson, however; it is better to introduce individual pupils to techniques of browsing while they are actually choosing books.

Choosing

While the children are choosing, the teacher can take the opportunity to talk to them. The things to talk about are:

the books themselves, what they are about, and how interesting they are likely to be.

the books children have read previously, what they thought of them, and what it was about them they liked or disliked.

what the children are generally interested in.

what kind of story a child wants to read this time.

This assumes that the teacher is familiar with children's books in general and with the books available in the school.

Shelving

There are ways of shelving books which will help children to choose.

1 Shelving by Topic —i.e., ghost stories, family stories, animal stories, etc. Pupils select from books within a theme, having decided what kind of story they want. The disadvantages of this are:

the difficulty of classifying the books.

it takes a good deal of time.

the classifiers have to know the books well.

2 Shelving by Author alphabetically. This encourages the habits necessary for using public libraries, is easier to handle for teacher and pupil, and provides more chance for the children of discovering unexpectedly interesting books than if they look only for animal stories, or any other topic.

The disadvantage is that keeping the books alphabetically is time-consuming, but this can be turned to advantage if children are involved. The practical task of reshelving books is an excellent way for the children to practice their alphabetical indexing skills.

3 Shelving in Levels enables the teacher to direct children to books appropriate to their reading ability, rather than allowing total free choice.

The disadvantage is that they can only follow their interests within the confines of any level and, because they are limited to a particular level until the teacher says they can move on, they can't choose books which will advance their reading.

A Coding System

If you shelve by topic or author, and code the books for reading level in unobtrusive ways, you will avoid the disadvantage mentioned above in 3. Code by a series of dots *inside* the back cover, with three broad groupings:

. up to reading age of six

.. from reading age six to eight and a half

... above eight and a half

The dots can be stamped inside the back cover using the eraser on the end of a pencil, and an ink pad. This is inexpensive and easy, and color-blind children will have no problems with it. Children who want to know how hard a book is can look at the dots.

A very simple strategy can be offered to pupils to test a book, to see if they will be able to read it:

Open at random, read a page, and every time you come to a word you can't read or don't understand, put down a finger. If at the end of a page you've got five fingers down, then it's probably a bit hard. On the other hand, if you want to read the book because of its topic, then risk it.

Double-checking this with the dot code can help the child to assess his or her own reading.

Advising the Children

Children will need to have the system explained to them. Putting it all down on paper in a simple way is very helpful, not just for the children, but for the staff and for parents too. Here is one example, devised for a multigraded class (8–9 year-olds), and presented to the children (see over).

Changing Levels

However a school organizes its reading program, decisions have to be made as to when a child is ready to tackle something new. One way of checking when the children are ready to advance is to offer them a book from the next level which the teacher thinks they will enjoy. If they cope with it, they can add another level to their area of selection.

Learning to Choose

From the very beginning of learning to read, children should be involved in making selections, even if only from a limited choice.

Making one's own decisions about which books to read is an important part of becoming a reader.

Learning when, and how, to reject books is equally important.

Being stuck on one book for any length of time develops poor attitudes toward reading: it becomes a chore rather than a pleasure.

Choice is not something that should be delayed as a reward for having learned to read. It is a central part of the process of learning to read itself.

How to Choose a Book to Read

1 *Find out where the books are*

Yellow Shelf. The print in these books is quite small and the books are either one long story with chapters like *The Hobbit* or a series of short stories like *The Power of Light* by Isaac Bashevis Singer or *Jessie's Ghost and Other Stories* by Barbara Ann Porte.

Red Shelves. These contain several series of books, for example: S. H. Burchard's sports star biographies, Schulz's *Peanuts* books, *Einstein Anderson* series, Jean Fritz's American history books. You'll find they're all clearly marked.

Wire Racks. One of these contains Easy-to-Read books and the other contains hard books from the public library, as well as our own *Dr. Seuss* books.

In both Mrs. M's area and Mr. B's area, there are books written by children for us all to read. If you borrow a book written by someone in your class, you must of course be very careful with it.

2 *Find out if you can read the book*

Do the five-finger test if you feel the book may be too hard. Begin reading the first page. Count the words that are too difficult for you. If they come to more than five on the page, the book may be too hard for you. Look for one that's easier.

If the book is too hard for you, but you like it all the same, ask your teacher if you can take it home for your mom and dad to read with you.

3 *Some more ideas*

a. Choose a book to take to read to the kindergarten class.

b. Choose the same book as your friend. Read it together and talk about it.

c. Choose a book that you already know. Books are often easier to read when you know the story first.

d. If you're reading a book of *short stories,* you don't have to read them in order. When you've finished one, go back to the contents page and choose another you think you'll like. There's no need to read them all, either. Just read as many as you want to, then choose another book. Or you could listen to the story on tape before you read it.

e. If you're reading a book that's gotten boring, or too difficult, either finish it quickly and choose another, or change it at once.

6
Introducing Children to Literature

Before a child can have an interest in reading, he must first have an awareness of it. The child who is unaware of the riches of literature certainly can have no desire for them.

Jim Trelease
The Read-Aloud Handbook

Making Fiction Important

Read Fiction Regularly to Your Class

Check on what stories the children have read or heard before.

Read at different times during the day. At the end of the day, there is no time to talk about the story and what it has meant to the children. Reading earlier in the day means that there is time to follow up on any interest or response.

When you have read a story to the class make available the book, books by the same author, and other books on the same theme.

When the book is a collection of tales about the same character (e.g., *Paddington, Frog and Toad*), read the first story and make the book available to the class.

Create a Reading Environment

Let the children see you reading and enjoying fiction.

Organize displays of fiction in the classroom and change them regularly. In creating new displays, consider both the books themselves, and the arrangement of the furniture and fittings. Make a feature of new books, books featured on television, programs such as *Reading Rainbow* etc.

Use posters to advertise books. Children who have read and enjoyed a book can design their own posters. Help them with the lettering by providing them with dry transfer lettering. Publishers have book jackets and posters available for their children's books. Some are free, while others are available at a nominal cost.

Make time during the day when every child (not necessarily at the same time) can spend half an hour reading fiction from the class or school library, the local library, or home.

Be Aware of Other Forms of Presenting Stories

Use stories tape-recorded by the teacher or produced by commercial companies. Set up listening centers where six to eight children may listen together without disturbing the rest of the class. Books on tape should be made available while children listen, or afterwards.

Use the Weston Woods slide or filmstrip versions of picture books to attract pupils' attention to particular stories. Slide/tape presentation can be very effective. There are also animated films of several books which can be shown in the classroom.

Build on the stories being broadcast on school radio, television presentations of serials, and programs such as *Reading Rainbow*. Find out in advance what is to be broadcast each term. The relevant books should be made available in the classroom.

Draw the Attention of Pupils and Parents to Fiction

Organize book fairs: that is, an attractive display of a wide selection of books which can be purchased. This is a way to involve parents actively in their children's reading.

Organize a school book store or book club where new and used books may be purchased or swapped.

Your local library (if there is one) is a valuable source and provides other services. Schools ought to make a positive attempt to introduce their pupils to the fiction books in libraries, to the libraries themselves, and to the librarian.

Make use of the services of school libraries not just for project books, but also for a selection of general fiction or displays to support something else.

Provide Fiction Books

Minimal provision of books to insure that all children have an adequate range to choose from is one hundred *titles* for every different class. In one year-group all the books can be available to the whole year. One hundred titles means there may be more than a hundred books because there may be more than one copy of each book. Ideally, fifty new titles should be added to the whole school stock each year.

At current prices, three to six paperbacks may be bought for the cost of one hardback, so a school ought to consider buying paperbacks among its stock. Plastic jackets can prolong the life of a paperback considerably.

Parents and pupils often want to present something to the school when they leave: it is a good suggestion for them to buy books for the school, and for the school to put commemorative bookplates inside the books to thank the givers.

Making Books Accessible to Children

Organize a Library Decisions have to be made about whether to have central libraries, class libraries or both. This decision can depend upon the design of a school: an open-plan school, for example, may find it better to organize a central place. A central library makes *all* books available to all children: the class library makes some available all the time. For most schools, a mixture of the two is best.

Library Periods Have regular library periods, probably weekly, of about 20–30 minutes in duration. During these periods pupils change their fiction books and spend time in silent reading. This should not be the only time when children can change books or read: it is, however, a time for the complete involvement of a class in reading, and perhaps of the teacher too. Those children who wish can listen to tapes of stories.

Browsing There are two major aspects of browsing: sampling from a whole collection of books, and sampling an individual book. Some of the reasons why we browse seem to be:

to discover generally what is available.

to see if that includes books of interest to us.

to isolate from the total collection books on particular subjects or by particular authors.

to sample individual books to get a taste of them.

to see if we want to read a particular book.

All habitual readers seem to browse, so it is a habit we want to encourage in children; they need the opportunity to browse through whatever books are available. Time for this should be created: it is too easy to expect it to happen of its own accord.

Involving Parents For parents of young children, it is valuable to make available a library of books that can be borrowed to be read to children at home, including those not yet in school. This is most needed when there is no source of books in the area.

By the time children reach the middle grades, they should be on the way to becoming independent readers and choosers; and parents should be involved in different ways. For example, booklists can be provided for Christmas and birthdays; parents can help to organize the school library, and so on.

Displays and Publicity To show children what is available and to make the books accessible, it is important to have a permanent display of books which is changed regularly.

New books should always be displayed for a time so that children can have their attention drawn to them, be encouraged to browse through them and to reserve them if they wish. Such displays can simultaneously demonstrate what is available in the school, and can also support particular things such as visits, topical events, radio and television series and serials, etc. Fiction and nonfiction books, posters, artifacts and anything else relevant should go into the display.

Borrowing Systems The systems should be as simple and efficient as possible. Whatever system is used, it will involve one person or a group of people in some work in designing and organizing it initially. The existing system should be explained to pupils. Your local library can offer advice to schools in organizing their systems. Parents and older children can help to run school libraries.

Making Sure Books Are Enjoyable

Check on Book Use

This can be done in two ways. Within the school, the books which are falling apart through use are probably popular. When reordering, order more copies of those. In addition, the public library and the school library will be able to give advice on which books are most popular and widely sought after.

Consult the Children

There can be a constant dialogue with the pupils about their favorite books, and books which they have read and enjoyed at home, or seen serialized on television. These discussions ought to inform book ordering.

Children can be asked to compile a list of recent and all-time favorites, a top ten, twenty or hundred books.

When you are reading publishers' catalogues and book reviews, include children in the decision-making.

Finding Out What Is Available

Some teachers already read and enjoy children's fiction, and this is the best way of knowing what there is. But for those who do not, there are strategies for learning about what is available, which make it possible to help pupils with their reading of fiction.

Provide time for teachers to visit publishers' exhibitions and book stores.

Involve all teachers in the selection of books when orders are submitted.

Display and preview in the staffroom all the new books arriving in school before they are distributed.

Post reviews of children's literature in the staffroom. Sources may include:

The Booklist (American Library Association)

Children's Choices, A project of the International Reading Association/Children's Book Council Joint Committee

School Library Journal, Best Books of the Year

Bulletin of the Center for Children's Books (The University of Chicago Press)

New York Times Book Review

The Horn Book

"Best Books" lists are published annually by organizations such as the Association for Library Service to Children of the American Library Association ("Notable Children's Books"); National Council of Teachers of English ("Teachers' Choices" and "Notable Children's Trade Books for the Language Arts"); International Reading Association ("Children's Choices").

Many libraries produce their own review publications.

Encourage staff to share new books and to review them for their suitability for reading aloud to a class.

Sharing Books with Children

As well as creating opportunities to find out what is available, teachers need time to share their own enjoyment of stories with their pupils. Teachers can:

tell or read a story to a "Parents and Toddlers Group." This will not only give pleasure to the toddlers but will introduce parents to the art of storytelling, or confirm parents' existing practice, so that they will continue to share that important activity with their sons and daughters.

"promote" new books when they are introduced to a class. The theme might be outlined, a passage read aloud, or illustrations enjoyed together.

take children along to the public library if there is one near the school. During the visit, while helping the children to find their way around, chat about what they've read and liked.

create opportunities for children to share the excitement of their reading. This is just as important as hearing children read, and the two can be combined if teachers encourage children to read them those pages which contain the most exciting passages.

Promoting Voluntary Reading

There are many other activities which encourage children to increase their voluntary reading. These include:

a regular "story spot" as part of the pattern of assemblies. Members of the staff may like to take responsibility for different weeks. The story session may incorporate music, slides, filmstrips or overhead projector transparencies, possibly produced by children, who may also illustrate the story through music, mime, movement or drama. After such sessions, copies of the book should be made available.

book clubs, which can foster good reading habits. There should be time to discuss the books presented, and for children to talk about other books they have enjoyed.

book fairs, an opportunity for children and parents to look at books together.

encouraging children to bring to school any books they are reading at home. Observations of what children are reading voluntarily can be most illuminating, and that kind of encouragement and sharing of reading experience may help other children to find more books they like.

encouraging pupils to talk in groups, or to the other children in the class, about any book they have enjoyed. There is little to equal peer endorsement.

All schools should have at least one member of the staff who is thoroughly versed in children's literature. That person should be used as a consultant by pupils and staff whenever they want to know more about books and stories. Ideally, all teachers should have the experience and enthusiasm to share stories with children.

Special Arrangements for Encouraging Reading

An increase in the provision of books to a school and in opportunities for pupils to encounter them always seems to increase book use. *Hooked on Books* reported by D. Fader and E. McNeil is a documented example of a literature-oriented reading program that "woke up" both teachers and students.

Another is Reading is Fundamental (RIF), a program sponsored by the United States Office of Education. RIF matches money raised by local schools for the purchase of books. For every dollar a school raises, RIF contributes three dollars. As a result, participating schools distribute free books to children three times a year. Enthusiasm abounds at RIF giveaways.

Helen Fleischman, an enthusiastic Long Beach school librarian, plans limerick, poster, bookmark, and author letter contests leading up to distribution day. On the actual day, Mrs. Fleischman has invited the local Congressman to speak, and has put on such plays about books as Beverly Cleary's "Sausage at the End of the Nose." She has encouraged both teachers and students to dress up as favorite book characters to the joy of both groups!

One of the underlying assumptions of RIF is that ownership of books is a factor in promoting a love of reading. Another important aspect of the program is the role parents play in it. Mrs. Fleischman has parents help with book selection and book distribution. The RIF newsletter shares ideas that help teachers, librarians, and parents build vibrant reading programs. (For more information write: RIF Program, 2500 L'Enfant Plaza, Washington, D.C. 20560.)

The effect of RIF is that children who weren't reading before start reading, and those who were already reading read even more.

These seem to be some reasons for the success of the program:

the provision of a very large number of books.

the fact that the books are informational, story, and picture books of high quality.

the regularity of the giveaways which children come to enjoy.

the fact that the children have an extended period of time to browse over and make their own personal selections.

the way the children waiting to make choices talk to each other and to their teacher about the books they have been considering.

above all, the factor of ownership. A child may say, "These are my books and I have read them all from cover to cover."

USSR: Uninterrupted Sustained Silent Reading

USSR represents a time during the school day when everybody in the school reads silently, children and adults alike. The best time has been found by many schools to be the beginning of afternoon school, and the time made available ranges from 20 minutes for the youngest readers to 45 minutes for 11-year-olds. For a discussion of USSR, see *The Reading Process: the teacher and the learner* by Miles V. Zintz (Wm. C. Brown Publishers, 1980).

Although the idea sounds curious at first, and many teachers, especially of younger children, are skeptical, those schools which have tried it find that after an initial period of training all children enjoy the time and seem to develop an interest in reading. The books read may be chosen from school or brought in from home if the children prefer. In one elementary school, the principal and secretary take their own little groups of children into the library or the reading area in the school entrance hall. A key characteristic of USSR is that no reports or assignments are required of readers as follow-up to their reading. The embryonic R.A.H.! R.A.H.! (Read at Home! Read at Home!) Project aims to accomplish the same things as USSR, except that parents serve as the reading models.

7
Reading for Meaning

When a child reads fluently he is succeeding in extracting meaning from the printed page. In particular, he is deriving meanings as close as possible to those intended by the author. Comprehension skills, as we see them, relate to various kinds of interaction between those meanings and the reader's purposes for reading.

A Language for Life: The Bullock Report (6.39)

The word "comprehension" has come to mean something relatively narrow, related to exercises designed to test an ability to explain a text or to answer questions on it. "Reading for meaning" implies a wider understanding of a text which involves *deriving meaning* in relation to the purposes for reading the text. "Reading for meaning," therefore, if it is to be fully successful, involves bringing together all the factors in reading:

understanding individual words, sentences, paragraphs, and texts.

the purposes for reading: whether the reader is seeking one piece of information, or reading for general interest or for pleasure, will control the way the pupil reads and understands.

Understanding

The Bullock Report suggests the following levels of comprehension:

literal: "the reader identifies material explicitly set down in the text." *para. 6.40*

inferential: "Here (the reader) interprets the significance of ideas or thoughts which might conceivably have been included or made explicit, but were not." *para. 6.41*

evaluative: "where the reader applies 'truth' tests to the material . . . to evaluate the internal logic of a passage, its authenticity, adequacy, and appropriateness." *para. 6.41*

appreciative: "the aesthetic equivalent of evaluation . . . the ability to respond to an author's use of language." *para. 6.41*

Although the various "levels" are separated here, in practice comprehension is a global activity, within which there is no separation of parts. Therefore, only "literal understanding" is treated separately below: the other levels—inferential, evaluative, appreciative—are brought together under the heading of "General understanding of texts."

Literal Understanding

In classroom terms, this implies that children can:

identify words and phrases in texts.
That is, that they are able to select the appropriate parts of a text to match what is required. It is possible to do this without understanding what the words or phrases mean, by using context and previous knowledge of language structures. For instance:

"Topological solutions are better than analytical solutions."

Q. Which solutions are better?

A. Topological solutions are better.

skim and scan successfully.
Both processes involve the reader in literal recognition—that is, recognizing that this word or phrase is the one being searched for.

identify the main idea in a passage.
To do this, pupils need to recognize previously identified key words.

organize information.
This ability (for instance in topic work) relies on children having the experience of exercising literal comprehension in practical, real life contexts.

Suitable activities for literal understanding:

using telephone directories.

using dictionaries.

reading labels in the classroom.

observing notices in public places.

reading timetables.

The Bullock Report comments:

Literal comprehension needs to be developed in a range of contexts where it is put to a practical purpose. . . . It is too important to be entrusted to exercises.
A Language for Life: The Bullock Report (8.15)

Literal comprehension questions are easier to set and mark than any other; they therefore tend to occur more often in published books and "laboratories." They are also easier to answer in writing. But they do not necessarily indicate that children have understood what they have read.

General Understanding of Texts

Children encounter different kinds of comprehension if:

they have several different kinds of printed material available to read.

they read for different purposes.

they are expected to do different things as a result of their reading.

Example

What controls the "levels" of understanding is the purpose for which the reader is reading. As an illustration, consider the following set of assignments for middle-grade students.

1. Using this matrix, determine what the various stores charge for computers.

	Computer Era	The Computer Factory	Interdynamics Data Systems
Apple IIc			
Macintosh			
Panasonic Sr. Partner			

2. What does each price include?
3. What peripherals does each computer have?
4. What is the memory capacity of each computer?
5. What software is available?
6. Consider these factors:

   the guarantees

   the repair service

   the convenience of purchase and service

Which store would you go to to purchase a computer?

In undertaking assignments of this kind, pupils may need to use other sources of information such as directions for telephone numbers, trade information, and streets; technical literature; and consumer guides.

Involvement in Normal Practice

The example of the advertisement assignment is of specially organized work; but all levels can be naturally involved in

normal classroom work. For instance, questions like these can be asked in casual talks with children at all times:

about reading books—

Do you remember what she/he said/did last time you read to me? *(Literal)*

about math books—

Are there any words there that mean the same as "divide"? *(Literal)*

about topic books—

Find out when the book was published. *(Literal)*

Have you seen anything on TV that is different from what is in the book? *(Evaluative)*

Do you think the author has ever seen a real volcano? (Inferential, evaluative)

Is there anything you wanted to find out that isn't there? *(Evaluative)*

about story books—

Before: *Have you read any other books by this author? What other books has he/she written?* *(Literal)*

Read the blurb and see if you will like it. *(Inferential)*

Open any page to read a few words: what do you think it will be like? *(Inferential, evaluative)*

After: *Which part did you enjoy most?* *(Evaluative)*

Who did you like best? *(Evaluative)*

Writing and Talking

It is usual for "comprehension questions" to be answered in writing. Research suggests that this is only valuable under certain circumstances. On the advertising assignment above, question 1 about the prices must be written, question 2 about fitting charges must be written, if you want to make comparisons. In both cases, the writing acts as a way of reorganizing and collecting information, copying out and bringing together parts that were originally separate. On question 3, the details about the stores may need to be written; the evaluation would be best done by pooling ideas and attitudes in group talk, and a different kind of writing might *follow* the talk.

As a general indicator:

Answers should involve *writing* when

information needs to be collected.

different chunks of information need to be stored or brought together.

the form *demands* that pen be put to paper: e.g., story, poem, table, diagram, etc.

Answers should be *discussed* when

they involve evaluation or judgment.

they involve emotional response to a story recently read (but note that some children would not want either to talk or to write about personal response).

they involve difficult or new ideas.

Purposes for Reading

An important aspect of reading behaviour is the ability to use different kinds of reading strategies according to the purpose and material. Consider the way one approaches the reading of different parts of a newspaper, advertising brochures, an income tax form or a railway timetable. The efficient reader will glance through selectively or scrutinize in detail. It is possible to read at various levels of intensity to match a particular purpose.

A Language for Life: The Bullock Report (8.18)

Normally in school it is the teacher who determines the purposes for reading, by suggesting topics, or asking questions to be answered from particular books. Too often the purposes suggested to children in school are very general: a child may be directed to "a topic on otters, or transport." Thus, the children are likely to read by simply going through a whole text, rather than searching for parts which are relevant to the purposes for which they are reading. To help children to become purposeful readers, certain procedures can be followed.

Step 1
Teachers can make their own purposes more explicit to the pupils. Instead of just suggesting "a topic on sea animals," ask them to find out about different kinds of whales from these books:

Simon—*Killer Whales*   Harper & Row

McNulty—*Whales: Their Life in the Sea*   Harper & Row

Step 2
When assignments are given (on worksheets or cards) make the search for information more realistic: instead of directing children to named books, or to specific pages in a book, make the search a valuable part of the activity. For instance, one might have assignments that look like these:

Find out about the artillery used in World War II using these books:

Edwin P. Hoyt—*Storm Over the Gilberts*

Bruce Bliven, Jr.—*The Story of D-Day*

Hodding Carter—*The Commandos of World War II*

Theodore Taylor—*H.M.S. Hood vs. Bismarck: The Battleship Battle*

find out about the origin of tank warfare.

OR

Find three books which tell you something about the eating habits of rabbits.

(Some schools insist that when pupils are involved in a topic, they must read at least three books. Children are then less likely to copy from one book.)

By working like this, pupils will need to use indexes efficiently, and to be able to skim to find the relevant passages. It is particularly effective for the teacher to select books in which there will be a conflict in the information so that pupils will have to evaluate the reliability of the books. However, some topics, in which the "facts" are less clear-cut (for instance, history, biology) will be easier to use than others where there is little possibility of finding conflicting evidence. Children of different ages will cope differently.

If the aim is to find information from a text, then the questions should be presented before the children read the text: when readers are alerted to what they need, their reading of the passage will be a purposeful search for the relevant information. If the aim is for the children to express *opinions* about the text, rather than recalling or retrieving information, then the questions may well follow the passage.

Step 3

When pupils are doing research for topics and so on, ask them first to make notes of what they already know about the subject. Then invite them to ask their own questions before they begin reading so that they know clearly what it is they are trying to find answers to.

In the outside world, readers normally have their own purposes that lead them to read. During a day, we all read many different materials:

a business letter.

a letter from a friend.

a newspaper.

weather summaries on TV.

circulars in the mail.

recipes.

road signs.

books.

Our responses to an individual piece of reading will depend on the purpose for which we read it. For example:

When the weather forecast appears on television we may watch it casually and forget it quickly; but if we are going to do something important the next day, we may scrutinize it very carefully.

We may read a circular in an offhand way, but if it happens to be about something of immediate interest—a wood stove advertisement in the middle of a cold spell—then we consider it in greater detail.

To prepare a meal for visiting friends, we need to read recipes and plan shopping and cooking on the basis of our reading.

Unless pupils acquire these skills while still at school there is a likelihood that the only approach they will ever use is inflexible, one-pace, line by line reading.
A Language for Life: The Bullock Report (8.18)

8

The Librarian in the Reading Program

Civilization, it was once said, is a race between education and catastrophe—and we intend to win that race for education.

John Fitzgerald Kennedy

Children still come to the elementary school library for the traditional purposes—to read, do research, and borrow books. But they also come to participate in book discussion groups, hear book talks, plan and perform puppet shows, read their original stories aloud, view films and filmstrips, and listen to cassette recordings. Today's school libraries are media centers and librarians are media specialists.

The Role of the School Librarian

Since librarians understand children's interests and needs and know books, they are in a unique position to contribute to children's reading success. By providing students with captivating books, they encourage and enrich reading. In effect, they are collaborators in the teaching of reading.

Through various organized and informal programs, librarians show students how important it is that they be equipped with the skills they will need to locate information, and how to have access to that knowledge. Because we live in an information society characterized by unprecedented social and technological change, this task is more vital than ever.

Librarians develop attention-attracting displays to arouse children's curiosity about many different subjects, organize book clubs focused on specialized interests, and generally make the library a center for finding things out.

The Librarian's Role with Children

The standard role of the school librarian is two-fold:

to guide children in reading for appreciation.

to show children how to use reference tools for researching information.

To accomplish the first goal, librarians provide happy experiences with books by sitting down with children and reading aloud to them. Children soon want to read books on their own, the prerequisite to learning how to read. Instilling the joy of reading is easy when librarians are also enthusiastic readers, because enthusiasm is contagious.

Further, in guiding students as they search for information, librarians know that learning to use reference tools must have meaning and purpose. They integrate learning library skills with specific research problems and classroom curriculum units. They advise children about how to locate the right book for their specific research requirements but, more importantly, they help make specific children independent enough to do future research on their own. To do this, librarians talk about these things with children:

the uses of a library.

behavior in the library—caring for books and being considerate of peers.

keeping the library a place children want to visit.

the basic arrangement of the library, including the location of books and various media.

the use of the card catalogues and the Dewey Decimal System.

the system for borrowing books.

the parts of a book.

operating audio-visual equipment.

reference skills.

developing critical reviewing skills.

judging and selecting suitable materials.

In addition, librarians compile schoolwide anthologies of poetry and/or favorite stories, including the books selected by school principals, school secretaries, and other staff members. They encourage groups of students to compile an annotated catalogue, which may be in booklet form, as an aid to book evaluation. They train children as library assistants to help with everyday chores, and find out their ideas about setting policy. Finally, they establish a "Writers' Corner" with handy supplies for those children who are inspired to get their own words down on paper.

Setting Up a Library That Invites Children to Spend Time in It

Libraries that invite children to spend time in them are physically comfortable. They may have thick carpeting to stretch out on, a bathtub of pillows to climb into, or a cushioned book nook to snuggle in. If adults enjoy reading while settled in well-worn armchairs or lounging on sofas, they will know that children enjoy a cozy environment just as much. Bulletin boards, both functional and provocative to stimulate reading, should meet the eye everywhere and be changed regularly. Work zones—centers for quiet reading, puppet shows, book discussion groups, a Writers' Corner, story time, or skills lessons—are clearly set off to keep children's conversation levels from disturbing others. Display cases hold "realia" such as student-made books, how-to books and student projects (e.g., samples of needlepoint, calligraphy, models), as well as bookmaking supplies (e.g., pencils, pens, inks, papers).

In libraries that invite children to spend time in them, children help to draw up the rules. Because they are asked to participate in making rules, chances are good that they will also abide by them. An open circulation desk can also be effective when children know their own responsibilities in checking out and returning materials.

Among the various projects that librarians can oversee to make the library inviting are:

1. *Literary Landmarks:* This is a semester-long undertaking in which the settings of books children have read are flagged on a large map of the world with the title of the book and the name of the reader.

2. *Book Ends:* Before they finish reading a book, children are encouraged to write an ending they think is satisfying. Then, they compare it with the author's.

3. *Teachers' Hobby Centers:* Teachers tell the librarian their hobbies and the librarian chooses and displays books for each of them. Students try to match teacher with hobby. A variation of this could be a display of books that were teachers' childhood favorites.

4. *Locale Letters:* Posted in a cardboard carton "mailbox," these letters and postcards—written from the land where the reader/traveler has journeyed in reading a book—tell about the people the reader has met, what the place was like, whether s/he had an enjoyable time, and so forth. Other travelers may read the letters before they embark on the same journey.

5. *Name the Author:* After reading or listening to thumbnail sketches of authors, including clues from bibliographic sources and book excerpts, children play at guessing their identities. Photocopied book jackets with blocked-out titles (taken from publishers' old catalogues) can serve as the focus of another game of identification.

6. *Poster Bookshelf:* Children can each draw or paint a bookshelf with empty shelves and fill it with "books"—strips of colored construction paper labeled with the author and title of books they have read (see figure 1).

THE NIGHT IT RAINED PANCAKES
by Mirra Ginsburg

Figure 1. Poster Bookshelf

To the student: Each time you finish reading a book, write the title and author on a strip of colorful construction paper and glue it to this bookcase. Watch how soon your shelves fill up as you read.

The Librarian's Role with Fellow Teachers

One of the most important tasks for librarians is that of elaborating upon the common reading experience of basals with related trade books. For example:

1. When children are reading only excerpts of a story in their basals, they often become interested in reading the entire selection. Part of E. B. White's *Charlotte's Web* appears in *Sea Treasures* (Scott, Foresman Reading, 1983) and Julia Cunningham's *Burnish Me Bright* in *Chains of Light* (Ginn, 1982). The story "A Kind of Magic," from Nina Bawden's *The Witch's Daughter,* appears in *New Frontiers* (Harcourt Brace Jovanovich Bookmark Series, 1983).

2. When children are reading selections by well-known writers in their basals, librarians might encourage them to read publishers' profiles of these writers and to discuss possible reasons why they wrote what they did. It will not be difficult for children to visualize Natalie Babbitt as a person after reading "The Eyes of the Amaryllis" (in *Green Salad Seasons,* Ginn, 1982); they will want to read some of her earlier works, such as *Tuck Everlasting* and *Kneeknock Rise.* Laura Ingalls Wilder's "Little Gray House in the West" (in *New Frontiers,* Harcourt Brace Jovanovich Bookmark, 1983) and the other "Little House" books reveal Laura's life from her early years through her marriage to Almanzo.

3. When children are reading selections in their basals which have also been presented in another medium, librarians can enrich their reading experience by providing them. Weston Woods produces fine quality sound filmstrips, nonverbal filmstrips, motion pictures, and recordings to enhance reading. Robert McCloskey's *Make Way for Ducklings* (in *Full Circle*, Macmillan Reading, 1983) is also a filmstrip with cassette. For "Ananse and His Visitor" by Edna Mason Kaula (in *Taking Off,* Lippincott Basic Reading, 1981), Weston Woods offers the filmstrip with cassette "Anansi the Spider" by Gerald McDermott, and Caedmon the cassette "African Village Folktales" (three volumes by Kaula). When children have read the lyrics to the song "My Favorite Things" by Oscar Hammerstein in *Catch the Wind* (Macmillan Reading, 1983) they will enjoy listening to the record of "The Sound of Music" or viewing the film.

4. When children are reading poems in their basals, they can read other works by the same poets. For example, "Nancy Hanks" by Rosemary and Stephen Vincent Benét (in *Close to the Sun,* Open Court, 1979) leads to *The Devil and Daniel Webster* (Archway, 1972), "Comma in the Sky" by Aileen Fisher (in *Blazing Trails,* Harcourt Brace Jovanovich Bookmark Series, 1983) leads to *Out in the Dark and Daylight* (Harper & Row, 1980), and "I'm Nobody" by Emily Dickinson (in *Soaring,* Lippincott Basic Reading, 1981) leads to *Poems of Emily Dickinson,* selected by Helen Plotz (Crowell, 1964).

5. When children are reading nonfiction in their basals, they can explore informational trade books on the same subjects for additional facts. The article "Tidal Waves" by Herbert S. Zim (in *Riders on the Earth*, Holt Basic Reading, 1980) opens the way for *The Big Wave* by Pearl S. Buck (Crowell, 1973), and the article "How to Make and Use a Cartridge Pinhole Camera" (in *Voyages*, Laidlaw Reading Program, 1980) introduces *Fun With Sun Prints and Box Cameras* (McKay, 1981).

6. When children are reading basal stories with a theme, a plot, or a setting which is similar to those in trade books, or specific literary genres—fairy tales, myths, fables—they can look for comparable tales in the library. "How the Camel Got Its Hump" by Rudyard Kipling (in *Ring Around the World,* Harcourt Brace Jovanovich Bookmark Series, 1983) points to *The Elephant's Child,* illustrated by Lorinda Cauley (Harcourt Brace Jovanovich, 1983), and the fables "The Monkey Tree" by William D. Hayes and "Coyote & Fox" by Kathryn Hitte (in *Turning Corners,* American Book Company, 1980) to *Aesop's Fables* by Ann McGovern (Scholastic, 1974), or the versions by Anne Terry White (Random House, 1963) or Heidi Holder (Viking, 1981).

These are only a few of the ways basal stories mesh with trade books; creative librarians can think of dozens more.

The librarian also does a number of things for and with fellow teachers:

1. Helps select and assemble the best of available teaching materials, including new books, films, cassettes, the times of relevant TV programs and dates, which are related to reading and literature.

2. Coordinates library resources with what is being taught in the classroom, bringing in book trucks of library materials to supplement ongoing special projects and units of instruction.

3. Enlists teachers' help in ordering new books and in recommending them to students (after reviewing responses to reading-interest surveys aimed to determine why particular children do not like to read, whether the home environment supports reading aloud, etc.).

4. Assists teachers by demonstrating to children research skills they will need in the classroom to perform specific tasks.

5. Helps with special class projects such as Book Week exhibits.

6. Reinforces and reaffirms the value of reading aloud by sponsoring read-aloud workshops and compiling read-aloud booklists.

7. Designs eye-catching bulletin boards for reading-related materials.

8. Keeps teachers up-to-date on book reviews related to special subject areas, or to monthly/weekly reading themes.

9. Shares games such as "Alphabet Search" (teams list items around the classroom for each letter in the alphabet), or "What's the Category?" (teams name as many insects, flowers, spices, bodies of water, etc. as they can).

10. Develops (and uses) media evaluation forms, which ask questions such as: In what ways do/don't the library resources meet the needs of the reading program? How are/aren't the library resources worthy of pupils' time and attention? Are concepts, format, vocabulary appropriate?

Librarians and teachers work together because they understand that the ultimate goal of a library-coordinated reading program is to enable pupils to be independent as they explore books for recreation and information, and that the library supplies the basic "content" for all aspects of the reading program.

The Librarian's Role with Parents

Although chapter 2 discusses the involvement of parents with reading, additional consideration of parents and the library is appropriate here. The emergence of Parents as Reading Partners Programs (PARP) is an acknowledgment of the importance of parents in the reading growth of their children, and as a supportive part of the total educational program. The proliferation of publications addressed to parents, such as "Helping Children Learn About Reading" (from The National Association for the Education of Young Children—NAEYC), which explains how parents can assist their infants, preschoolers, and school-age children to prepare for and enjoy reading, is further evidence. The librarian's work with parents is important and has several facets.

First of all, librarians help parents to appreciate and encourage the breadth of their children's reading interests. Parents need to know that their children may be simultaneously reading formidable-looking books and paperbacks and comics, depending upon their interests and the needs of the moment. The most supportive parents are those who refrain from criticizing children's varying reading tastes, because they understand that readers of an abridged, comic-illustrated version of a book such as *The Prince and the Pauper* will often go on to seek the Mark Twain original.

Second, librarians encourage family reading and sharing of books. In the interest of reviving "the good old days," when children found comfort on a warm lap, listening to a wonderful book, they distribute read-aloud bibliographies and hold read-aloud workshops for parents, which are frequently sponsored by PTA committees. Such committees serve as liaisons with parents and through newsletters or flyers they make available "New Books" columns and other pertinent information. They arrange for speakers to celebrate special days, such as Hans Christian Andersen's birthday or International Book Week, and hold book fairs or assist the librarian with RIF (Reading Is Fundamental) book giveaways. Both groups working together alert families to high quality movie or television versions of books, but remain delighted when children say they "like the book better."

In addition, librarians meet with parents to help them select books for their children and develop a home library so children will realize that books do not belong only in schools or public libraries. They encourage parents to purchase bookplates for their children's very own books. All children should have their own books, and attractive bookplates, whether home made or professionally printed, call special attention to that ownership.

Librarians talk with parents about the purposes literature serves for all of us: to communicate cultural values, present contrasting life experiences, and tell us about the world and its people. They recommend that parents give their children books and magazine subscriptions as gifts. Both know that some books they loved in childhood might be as out-of-date today as the quill pen, so they are careful in selection. But by giving their children books, parents show them just how much they themselves prize reading.

Finally, parents may participate actively at the school library by helping to reshelve books, reading aloud to small groups, or taking children's dictation in the Writers' Corner. In these ways, parents complement the librarian's important role in mediating their children's reading experiences.

9

Reference and Study Skills

Pupils should learn how to organise their reading, firstly by being able to locate, evaluate and select the material they need, and secondly by applying organised study methods to the material itself.

A Language for Life: The Bullock Report (8.13)

Organizing Resources

Some things can be learned once and for all, so that when pupils have learned to use indexes, or to survey source material, and so on, they will know how to do it. But the ability to make use of available resources depends on the way these particular resources are organized, so pupils will have to become familiar with each new system they encounter.

If resources are collaboratively organized by the whole school, then it is the school's responsibility to help children to acquire knowledge of what and where the resources are, and how they are organized. If individual teachers make their own arrangements in their own classroom, then each teacher will have to take on that responsibility individually.

Available Resources

All schools have a wide variety of available resources, which include:

printed materials.

audio-visual and electronic equipment and microtechnology.

software for the above: tapes, records, slides, etc.

what librarians and archivists call "realia" (that is, artifacts and natural objects).

essential equipment that must be stored but be accessible—rulers, papers, scissors, etc.

To be able to explain to children how the resource system works, the school or individual teacher must be clear about the basic principles by which the resources are classified and organized. The main point is that the system should be *efficient*—that is, users should be able to find out what they want without difficulty. A system may be so personal that although the teacher who devised it is clear about its structure, children or other teachers may find it hard to use.

Designing a System

The conceptual framework of a resource system is the set of basic principles which controls where items are entered and how they are described.

This framework is best sorted out by the staff together so there is some kind of continuity in the school. Once the basic principles have been thought out, the system can be tested by checking how a pupil would locate typical information, for instance:

how to feed a racoon.

the identification of a fossil.

a book by Natalie Babbitt.

something about sanitation workers.

the record of the music from "The Nutcracker."

If everyone can successfully agree how the resources to answer those questions would be found, then it's safe to assume that the system can be explained to pupils.

If the system is devised by one teacher, then it is important that *all* the staff should be involved in trying it out. Everyone will have to use the system, so everyone should be *able* to use it. The system should be devised as much from children's questions as from staff questions. A staff that is beginning the process of devising a system can collect the kinds of questions their pupils have recently asked, and use them as the starting point.

Storage

Physical storage is a practical problem that depends on the space and storage facilities available in an individual school. As long as pupils know where to find things, these problems can be solved.

Central storage is not essential as long as the cataloguing system indicates clearly where things can be found, and as long as the movement of pupils to the resources does not interfere with normal school activity.

Defining Resources

A school's resources can be described and listed under these headings:

books, fiction and nonfiction.

pamphlets, leaflets, brochures, timetables, etc.

pictures, maps, archive documents.

equipment—tape recorders, video recorders, Language Masters, etc.

tapes, slides, records.

electronic data-bank and microprocessors.

calculators and electronic games.

natural and industrial objects (e.g., fossils, car engines).

math and science apparatus.

commercially produced materials, kits, "laboratories" etc.

different types of reference books (decisions need to be made about which ones to make available).

dictionaries.

atlases and street directories.

encyclopedias.

thesaurus (either Roget or others).

telephone directories.

yearbooks, almanacs.

The other major location of resources is external to the school— in libraries, museums, and the community in general. Information on resources outside the school can be kept in the central catalogue.

Organizing the Library

Most schools find that they have to organize nonfiction books centrally because they cost too much to equip each class separately. The system employed in the library should provide a framework for continuity throughout the school as children get older.

Some schools use a modified Dewey system, which shelves books according to subject and allocates base numbers to each classification. The full Dewey system uses from one to four decimal points after the base number; for instance, "Wildlife conservation organizations" are classified as 333.906. But the primary school may well use only a selection of the base numbers. For example, "Plants, trees and flowers" are all included in the modified Dewey base number 580; "Animals and birds" are 590. By grade 6, "Animals and birds" may be subdivided. A book on spiders will be found under 595, books on fishes under 597, birds 598, mammals 599.

In an elementary school the shelf can have a general label, for instance "Animals and birds 590," but within it the books can be arranged and numbered with their appropriate base numbers. Thus both older and younger children can use the same library.

Color-coding is sometimes used to classify a library, but there can be many more categories than colors available, and color-blind children find it difficult to use such a system.

Teaching the System

The following is an outline of a general approach designed to help children to acquire the necessary knowledge of available resources.

Know what's there yourself.

At the beginning of the year, spend time explaining the organization to the children. Some points may need stressing:

where a/v equipment is stored and how it can be borrowed.

where essential implements and apparatus are normally stored, and the system for using and returning them.
This applies to things like rulers, scissors, paste, etc.

what is stored centrally and what is available in the classroom.

Make available something on paper which summarizes where things are, how to find them, how to borrow them, and how to return them.

Provide some exercises designed to insure that the children understand and can operate the basic system. For instance:

Find me a book by Joan Aiken.
Find me two books that have pictures of goldfinches.
Put this dictionary back on the shelves.
Return this record.

Exercises like this should be organized for small groups rather than the whole class, and the assignments should be different so that only a few children want each resource. Exercises like these should not need to be continued for very long.

It is important to move away quickly from exercises, and to introduce work that will necessarily require children to use the resources. The resources should not be previously chosen by the teacher and presented to the children; the search for them is an important part of learning what's available and how to use it.

Monitor constantly the way children are using the system. This can be done by:

watching how they use the resources.

asking what difficulties they have had.

noting which questions they could not find answers to.

If they could not find answers to the question, was it because—

the system is not efficient enough?

the resources are not there?

the pupils are not proficient enough in using the system?

it was the wrong question?

The monitoring can probably only be done generally; but at the end of a topic, or the end of a term, a teacher can valuably discuss these points with a group or a class.

Introduce older pupils to the systems being used in public libraries and museums: discuss the differences between the categorization used by these outside places and by the school.

Reading for Topic Work

In elementary schools, it is mainly in topic work that children use reference materials to define an area of search. Some topics result from children formulating their own questions, to which they want answers. Sometimes, a teacher will suggest topics to the children individually, or children select one because topic work is required of them. Sometimes a topic for a year group or for the whole school will be planned by the staff.

Asking Questions

When pupils formulate their own questions, the questions are likely to be highly specific, for instance:

What sort of fossil is this?

How does a car engine work?

Is it true that if you eat raisins, you get appendicitis?

How do these electronic television games work?

Here, they begin with the specific, but will move out toward the general as they begin to find answers to their questions.

When a topic is organized by the school or the teacher, there are not likely to be such specific questions: instead, the theme is very general, and it is sometimes difficult for pupils to cope with such generalizations as "communications," "transportation," and so on.

When a teacher begins with a general field of inquiry and finds a way of identifying specific areas that can be usefully handled by a primary school child he or she is "defining an area of search."

Defining the Area in a Self-Chosen Topic

When the topic is one that children have devised for themselves, then one way of beginning the process of defining the area of search is for the child to answer these questions:

What do I know already about this topic?

What do I want, or need, to know?

How can I find out?

The teacher will need to help or advise with the last question. Questions like these help a child to narrow down the possibilities. A question that begins by being unanswerable, like "Why are the leaves different on different trees?" can be reduced to one that is answerable: questions that want to know *why* are much harder to find answers to than questions that want to know *about*.

Defining the Area in a Teacher-Chosen Topic

When teachers make the decision about what topics should be, the topics tend to begin very generally, and pupils will have to define their area of search in these ways:

Read a general book to make a survey of basic facts and background, and to study pictures, diagrams, etc.

Move from that to specific books, depending on the previous general reading. This second-phase reading will locate and isolate possible areas that will need further research, and will increasingly refine the questions that are asked. The use of bibliographies and footnote references in these books will help in the search for more specific areas.

It should be noted that topic books that lack bibliographies, indexes, and the usual aids of information books, are unhelpful. When a school wants to spend money on books, the presence or absence of these things can be useful indicators of the quality of an information book.

Answer detailed questions:

using other books in the same classification.

turning to catalogues to locate more specialized resources.

using indexes, chapter headings, content pages, to search for special information.

Using a Subject Index and Classified Catalogue

A *subject index* tells the searcher where to look in general in a resource system. A *classified catalogue* lists individual items.

The Subject Index

A subject index contains the names of topics in the library or the total system, presented in alphabetical order. It shows the user where to look for information on a topic.

Subject indexes may be compiled by the children themselves in their own classroom. Follow this procedure:

the children list topics that interest them.

they put the topics in alphabetical order; the teacher helps if necessary.

they assign a location to each topic.

For younger children the index may be a wallchart, for older children a card-index system can be introduced.

Thus an entry for young children may read:

> ANIMALS: Books—shelf 590
> Records—A13
> Slides—C9

For older children the index may also refer the searcher to the classified catalogue which gives more detailed information about books in the library.

The Classified Catalogue

The classified catalogue lists individual items in the collection, arranged in the order of the classification system, so that the searcher can relate the order in the catalogue to the order of storage. For example under 591 in the full Dewey system, the searcher will find in the catalogue all the books about mammals:

591.90944 *The Cave: What Lives There* by Andrew Bronin (Coward)
591.92 *Animals of the Sea* by Millicent Selsam (Four Winds)
591.994 *Animals of Australia* by Maurice Burton (Abelard)

Using the System

The only efficient way for pupils to develop an understanding of subject indexes is to use them in the ways outlined above. The pattern to be followed is:

introduction to the system.

exercises to help children become familiar with it.

real use as soon as possible.

For the exercises, one might try things like:

How many books have we got about birds?

Who wrote our copy of *The Lore and Legends of Flowers*?

Where would you look for a book on pirates?

Surveying Source Material

Once a child has located the general area of books or resources, the importance of selecting the right material is obvious. A child should not just use any book on the chosen topic: the question is to find the most appropriate one.

Before a reader skims and scans, he or she should survey the material and consider the author, following a few simple procedures. This, or a simplified version of it, can be displayed on a poster in the classroom, library, corridor or hall.

What are the author's credentials for writing on this topic?

Are there initials after the name?
(For example, U.S.N. (Rtd.) for books on ships.)

Has he or she practical experience in this field?
(For example Seymour Simon on science.)

Is there a biography of the author? What can we learn from it?

What is the date of publication?

Teachers will need to show children how to read the printing history of a book (usually printed on the reverse of the title page). If it was written some time ago, has it been revised?

Different books on the same topic may have very different dates—for example, a book on dinosaurs written in 1960 will probably be very different from a good book on them written today.

In some topics such as world geography, space explorations, sports, electronics and computers, the date is crucial.

What books or sources has the author used in producing this book?

Children are not always aware that many children's information books are derived from other books, and are not firsthand work; errors or misinformation can be perpetuated.

Children should learn to be suspicious of any book that does not have a bibliography or acknowledgements, unless it is clearly based on actual experience.

Does it look as though the book is likely to be helpful and interesting?

A quick skim through, looking at points like chapter headings, illustrations, diagrams and, above all, the index, should become basic practice for all book users.

If children are to be able to survey source material, teachers will need to explain bibliographies to them, and help them to assess the date and authors of the books they have chosen.

Skimming and Scanning Skills

Finding the Right Book

The process of finding the right book for their purposes involves pupils in knowing clearly what their purposes are, and then testing the books by skimming through them.

Skimming is defined as "a rapid style used mainly to establish what the text is about before deciding whether and where to read" (*The Effective Use of Reading,* Lunzer and Gardner, 1979); and also as reading where "the eye travels quickly down the page, almost as if hunting for the salient points of the passage" ("Reading to Learn," Patricia Wright, in *Reading Today and Tomorrow,* ed. Melnick and Merritt, 1972).

Finding the Right Place

When pupils have found the right book, they have to locate the information they need. Some pupils who have not been shown how to skim and scan find it laborious to locate specific information because they do not tackle the job systematically. There are still children who, at the age of fourteen or fifteen, start at page one and try to read through the whole book to find what they are looking for, rather than skimming or scanning quickly to find the place they need.

Scanning is hunting for the right place. What happens is that, "when information of apparent importance is found, the pace slows, and the reader attends a little more closely to the immediate context." ("Reading to Learn," Patricia Wright, *ibid*). Scanning, then, is reading quickly to see if a point is present in the text, or to locate it so that one can read it with attention.

Teaching Skimming and Scanning

Children should be shown how to locate the required section of text without having to read through the whole book. To do this, they will need firstly to be clear about what they are trying to find. Then they can be introduced to the following procedure:

Use the contents page or list of chapter headings.

Does it contain the appropriate points you are looking for?

Use the index to see if the topic is represented in the book.
Children often need training in the use of indexes. For instance, a pupil who wants information about the eye of a dragonfly from a general book on insects will need to appreciate that it should be looked for under "dragonfly" rather than "eye." At first, pupils may not be aware that indexes move from the general to the particular.
They will also need to learn how to recognize the relative importance of index entries.
Faced with the entry:
Stagecoaches 7, 11n, 24–31, 71
pupils need to know that they should look at pages 24 to 31 first, and that page 11 is probably not important, because stagecoaches are only mentioned in a footnote.

Use all the cues available.
Children will need to have their attention drawn to what these cues are.

In skimming:

pictures, illustrations and diagrams demonstrate something about the general topic and its treatment.

chapter titles, page headings, subtitles, guide words (in dictionaries and encyclopedias) all offer rapid ways of assessing topics.

In scanning:

words in boldface, italic, or capital letters.

subheadings in the text.

first sentences in paragraphs and sometimes last sentences.

the occurrence of key words, that is, the appearance of a relevant word or group of words: for instance, in a search for information

about a dragonfly's eye, words like "vision," "sight," or "lens,"
will lead us to dwell on this part of the text.

Practicing the Skills

Children will use their skimming and scanning skills in the course of a normal school day if the teacher has designed assignments which necessarily involve reading for real purposes, for example, to discover the diet of mice, in order to feed new pets.

The best practice is for pupils to select their own materials with the teacher's help and encouragement when they are needed. Pupils can develop their understanding of the whole process if they are encouraged to talk through their search for the right material. For instance, pupils can be asked, individually or collectively:

how they found the right books.

how they knew the book contained suitable material.

if books were rejected as unsuitable, and why.

how specific passages were found, or how they intend to find them.

Although it is easier, and apparently saves time, if children are told which pages of which book to turn to, it will, in fact, prevent them from practicing their skills of skimming and scanning.

Assessing a Child's Competence

The best way of assessing a child's competence in coping with these reference and study skills is through the kind of discussion described above.

Observations could be made and noted of each child's strengths and weaknesses, and the weaknesses should become the areas on which further experience should be given.

It is less useful to assess this area by test or assignment card: what matters is whether children use skimming and scanning in actual research work.

Since reading is a major strategy for learning in virtually every aspect of education it is the responsibility of every teacher to develop it. It is difficult for most teachers to be fully aware of the complexity of these skills. This explicit awareness *is* necessary, for left to their own devices many pupils develop poor reading habits and others do not achieve the efficiency of which they are capable.

A Language for Life: The Bullock Report (8.9)

10

Assessing Progress
in Reading

Few areas in the primary curriculum receive as much scrutiny as reading. In some parts of the curriculum—for instance, discussion, music, art, science—we seldom make any attempt to assess a child's progress. Reading is different:

Teachers feel they must keep a check on their pupils' progress.

"Reading standards" are often the subject of debate in the media.

It is the area where parents experience the greatest concern.

Some reasons for constantly checking pupils' performance in reading might be:

"Because they're there," that is, because there are more tests available for reading than for anything else, this seems to suggest that reading needs to be tested frequently.

A need for benchmarks, that is, the natural desire for any teacher to know how successful the teaching is, and how well the children are progressing.

The need for an objective check on subjective opinion. Public systems of evaluation carry more weight with teachers than their own personal, informal opinions.

Accountability. The desire to be seen to be achieving one's aims, and to point to achievements in reading as proof that the school is doing its job.

Recognition of the importance of reading, which is probably seen by the public as the most important thing an elementary school has to teach.

Because of the last two points—accountability and public importance—schools feel pressure on them, from parents, from school boards, and from "society," all of which lead to the feeling that we must keep a constant check on performance in reading, so we can justify ourselves to anyone who asks.

Five Systems of Assessment

The main systems commonly used by schools to keep track of their pupils' reading are:

1 The standardized reading test.
2 The reading series itself, and progress through it.
3 Formal and informal observation.
4 Diagnostic teaching.
5 A record of books read.

Before we use any system of assessment, we should be clear about what aspects of reading it is attempting to deal with. For instance, word recognition tests (like Schonell and Burt) test a child's ability to say a word out loud. The reader does not have to be familiar with the word or understand its meaning—just to pronounce it correctly. This "sounding out" is a process that is necessary in reading aloud, but it is not clear how essential it is to the fluent silent reading which is the main aim of our teaching. If we want to find out how well a child copes with a text and derives meaning from it, a word recognition test will not give us that information.

1 The Standardized Reading Test

Reading tests in general use may be categorized as follows:

Prereading Competence tests (e.g., Clymer-Barrett, Harrison-Stroud, Lee-Clark, Metropolitan Readiness). These are tests in which children are evaluated for visual and auditory discrimination, sentence copying, alphabet knowledge, etc.

Word Recognition tests (e.g., Gilmore, Gates-McKillop, Gray, Botel, Slossen, San Diego Quick Assessment). These tests evaluate rate and accuracy of oral reading, phonics mastery, meaning vocabulary, etc.

Vocabulary tests (e.g., subtests of the reading achievement portion of the Stanford Achievement Test, the Metropolitan Achievement Test, and the SRA Achievement Series). These tests measure both the student's understanding of key vocabulary and ability to decipher the word.

Comprehension tests (e.g., Nelson, Iowa Basic Skills, Gates-MacGinitie). These tests measure pupils' skill in understanding connected reading in short paragraphs. The paragraphs are graduated in difficulty from simple to more difficult which test advanced skills.

Most of the tests produce a "reading age"; some claim to produce a diagnostic profile.

The manuals are generally careful to define the limitations and possible uses of the test, but there is a tendency to assume that the score on one test is comparable to the same scores on other tests; that is, to assume that 8.4 on Nelson represents substantially the same reading achievement as 8.4 on Gates-

MacGinitie, and that both mean that a child has the reading ability of an average child aged about eight. A more dangerous assumption is that "8.4" means that the child has the *intelligence* of an average eight-year-old.

Reading tests are the most common instrument used to examine children's reading, but they may not be the most efficient way of finding out how well children can read.

2 The Basal Readers

Most reading series are constructed and used on the assumption that Book 4 is "harder" than Book 3 and "easier" than Book 5, and therefore, that to read it, children must be better at reading than they were when they read Book 3. The movement through the series is seen as representing a developmental progression, and the child's move from book to book, or from level to level, as indicating progress. For many schools, the *record* of what is read is used to assess progress. The assumption is that the ticks which represent completed books also represent "progress" in generalized reading ability.

Most series are internally consistent, so that Book 12 is clearly an advance on Book 6 in some way—harder or longer words, longer sentences, more words to the page, and so on. But care is needed about the comparability between different series: Book 3 in various series may represent quite different kinds of reading demand for children.

An increasing number of schools are organizing their reading program in *levels,* which means that children will read several books at one level before moving on to the next one. When a program is organized like this, and there is no obvious linear progression from book to book, it becomes necessary to look for an effective way of evaluating the children's reading.

3 Formal and Informal Observation

All teachers naturally and constantly observe their children, and could make valid comments on their reading attainment from these observations. Some examples may illustrate this.

Teacher A (children of 4–7 in the same class) Children may choose to read a book into a tape recorder. The tape recorder is located in a "reading corner," outside the classroom, and the books available are a mixture of published series books and appropriate "real" books. They are sorted into boxes of roughly the same level, and the children can read any book of their choice. The book they choose is the first point of note for the teacher: what they *choose* to read is a significant indication of their interests and abilities.

Children who want to record their readings (not all of them do) have their own tape, and read for as short or long a time as they choose. The tape can be taken home for parents to listen to. The teacher listens to the tape later, and can see how the children have tackled the problems they meet during the reading, what kind of problems they had, and what strategies they use in their reading. Above all, the teacher learns how they cope without any help. S/he learns, among other things, that some children who appear to be weak readers when they are reading to her/him, perform much better when they are reading into the tape recorder. The strategy is perhaps the closest one can get to eavesdropping on the normal silent reading of children.

Teacher B (6–7 year-olds) makes a point of watching the children for at least twenty minutes a day, paying particular attention to their behavior with books—which of them choose reading as an activity, how they select a book from the book corner, and so on. The teacher talks to one boy who wants to read his project aloud, and asks him where he found some of his information. As he answers, the teacher notices he can:

find on the shelves the two books he used for his project.

find quickly the pages he used.

show the passages in the originals he used, and explain how he changed them in his text.

The teacher concludes that he is well on the way to being proficient in general book use and in early research skills and decides to try him out on index use and other reference work.

Teacher C (9–10 year-olds) asks the children to read their books to themselves before they come to the teacher about them. When it is their turn, the teacher does not ask them to read aloud, but instead talks to them about what they have read, asking questions like:

which part did you like best?

when this happened, what did you think about it?

what did you think this part meant?

what are you going to read next?

what have you liked reading best so far?

Their time together is completely occupied by talk. As the children talk about their reading, the teacher discovers how well they have understood the books they chose.

Teacher D (11–12 year-olds) A group is provided with individual copies of an appropriate reading book, and reads silently, beginning at the first page. By observing them the teacher notes:

which pupils move their lips, follow with their fingers, or use rulers or paper under the lines.

which pupils concentrate on reading for the whole of the fifteen minutes.

which pupils seem disaffected by reading (or simply dislike this book).

which pupils struggle but persevere, and which struggle and give up.

After fifteen minutes, they stop and the teacher records the number of pages read by each pupil. That record gives a very rough indication of the pupil's speed of reading and/or interest in the text. In addition, by asking them to read the book in their own time, the teacher can note which pupils actually finish the book. It is not uncommon, for example, for pupils with low scores on reading tests to read surprisingly complicated books which catch their interest. Thus, a 12-year-old girl who was considered a very poor reader nonetheless read *Little House on the Prairie* with such enthusiasm that she carried on to read the remainder of the series.

An informal assessment like this can also be made of non-narrative reading. The teacher may make additional observations here, such as which pupils turn back to reread, which use the index, dictionaries and follow up other references. (See *Assessing Children's Language*, A. Stibbs (1980) Boynton/Cook).

In all cases, the teachers' observations are in addition to any other more formal or standardized system of evaluation; their observation forms a natural part of their everyday behavior, a way in which they constantly review and monitor what their children are doing.

Using Children's Own Comments Valuable information which is of direct use to teachers may be discovered by asking children to comment, either in writing or discussion, on questions like:

what kinds of reading do you like to do?

what kind of reading do you find difficult?

what stories do you like best/least?

what has helped you most to learn to read?

do you read different things at school? at home? during the vacation? during the summer/winter?

what kinds of book would you like to read?

Children who have read a particular story or book can be put together, without the teacher, but with a tape recorder, to talk about their responses to what they have read, or what they feel they have learned from it.

There is evidence that when children have the opportunity to speak freely about their reading, they approach it in ways that show adults the very different approaches that children use in understanding what they read; and also, that free talk *helps* them to understand it better.

4 Diagnostic Teaching

Some activities are intrinsically interesting, are themselves valuable, and are also ways in which the teacher can learn important things about the children's reading abilities. Some of these activities are cloze procedure, prediction and sequencing, and the use of informal reading inventories. The teacher uses the activities not to test the children to see whether they get things right or wrong, but to observe what they do, how they do it, and what the teacher can learn about the children and their educational needs.

Cloze Procedure The reader is asked to read a prepared passage from which certain words have been omitted. One or two paragraphs of the original are left untouched so that the readers can get the feel of the writer's style and the meaning of the passage. Cloze paragraphs may be constructed by:

omitting every fifth or eighth word, for example. The more frequent the deletion, the harder the passage is to read.

omission of selected words, e.g., nouns or prepositions, or words that are crucial to the meaning of the passage for some reason.

The children can deal with the passage in different ways:

deciding in group discussion what words should fit the gaps.

completing the passage as individuals before coming together in groups to decide on an agreed version.

The important point is that the teacher should not insist on a "right" answer. The children decide on the most appropriate word, given the context, and what they already know. It may well be that their choice of the most appropriate word is better than the original. The role of the teacher is to invite the children to compare the suggestions made, to invite explanation of why they were made, and to enable the group or the class to decide on what is felt to be the most appropriate choice.

By observing the strategies that children use to decide what words fill the gaps, by noting the occasions when children apparently miss the point of context and put in something completely inappropriate, and by seeing what sense is made of the passage as a whole, the teacher can have a valuable picture of the approach of individuals to reading and understanding continuous texts.

Prediction and Sequencing In prediction, a story or passage is read aloud, or given to the children, one paragraph at a time. After each paragraph, the children discuss what they think will come next in the passage. In sequencing, a passage is prepared by being cut into its constituent sentences or paragraphs. The children have to arrange them in an appropriate order.

Both prediction and sequencing are best carried out in small groups of three to eight children. During the discussion, they will be drawing particularly on their anticipation of what is *most likely* to come next, but they will also note that as more of the passage is revealed it becomes easier to predict what *will* come next, rather than what *might* come.

In both, they have to be alert to cue-words, like "therefore— however—on the other hand—when . . . ," and need to be able to draw on their knowledge of the way books are structured, and the way stories and arguments are constructed.

By taping the discussion, the teacher will gain insight into the strategies the children use to solve reading problems. Because the work is done in groups, the children can learn from each other, and the teacher can draw the class's attention to the way they have worked.

The Informal Reading Inventory Because many teachers have felt unhappy about using single sentences to assess children's reading, and have been cautious about standardized tests, the informal reading inventory, which does not disrupt ordinary teaching, has been found useful.

Passages are selected from the child's everyday reading material: no special material is needed. The children are asked to read the passage in two ways:

Aloud—so that the teacher can check the reader's *accuracy*.

Silently—after which the teacher can check on the reader's *un-*

derstanding. The reading aloud does not in itself show if the child can understand the text.

During the reading aloud, the teacher may systematically note miscues, or any feature of the child's performance that seems worth noting. During the checking for understanding, the child may be able to look back at the passage, or have to answer without rereading. Questions should cover the full range of comprehension.

If a score is wanted, the passages can be selected in chunks of 100 words. Then a count of words incorrectly read will give a percentage score for accuracy. If there are ten questions, then that gives a second percentage score for understanding. It is assumed there are three levels at which children may read (Pumfrey, 1976).

Independent—the level at which children will cope successfully with most reading, and will solve their own problems.
The score that indicates this level is
99–100% accuracy.
90–100% understanding.

Instructional—a level at which the child may need some help to cope. The expectation is that with assistance, the child will become an independent reader.
The score that indicates this level is
95–98% accuracy (that is, no more than five words read incorrectly).
70–89% understanding (that is, at least seven questions answered correctly).

Frustrational—the level at which the material is too difficult for the child, or the child is unable to cope for some reason.
The score that indicates this level is
Less than 95% accuracy.
Less than 70% understanding.

5 A Record of Books Read

The teacher normally keeps a record of books read by the child who is "on the basal." If children are reading other books they can be encouraged to record what they read.

It is also an advantage if the child records the books which have been read to him or her, because it can be a useful topic of discussion between the teacher of a new class and the child. It is valuable for the teacher to set aside time to talk to children about what they are reading at home. This can be as helpful as the conventional hearing of a child reading a page or two.

Teachers can ask parents what their child is reading or has had read to him or her at home, including material other than books. Membership in the library can also be discussed with parents, who can give a very clear picture of the total reading pattern of their child.

Older children can fill in a proforma such as the following example at intervals to indicate their current reading habits:

Date	Title and author of book	Source	No. of pages read	No. of times read	Comment

Such a record can give an illuminating picture of a pupil's reading experience. As an example, on p. 100, is a record kept by a 12-year-old girl, Jane.

The handwriting and the notes on the books give the impression of an inefficient, perhaps inadequate reader. But the record in fact shows that Jane is poised to become a successful reader. She wants to read *The Water Babies* but is put off, presumably by the style and slowness of the opening pages. She has, though, coped successfully with *Little House on the Prairie*, perhaps encouraged by the television series, and is enthusiastic about reading the rest of the series. Since most of the books she reads come from the class library, the importance of the choice offered by the school and her teacher is clear. With help from the teacher—like making certain the other "Little House" books are available, and perhaps helping her to cope with *The Water Babies*—Jane might manage to do what she seems to want to do—to read fiction. Where a reading test or a casual judgment might have dismissed her, the record shows the growth points in her experience.

Other records from the same class show that good records are always informative. Nicola's list contains 17 books rather than Jane's 6; but the pattern is just as interesting. She shows us a girl poised on the edge of adolescent and young adult reading, but not yet certain enough to take the plunge. So she enthuses about John Rowe Townsend's *The Intruder* and Russell Hoban's *The Mouse and His Child,* two complex books, and rejects Betsy Byars's *The House of Wings* as being "Not a very good book"; but also enthuses about *Charlotte's Web* and Enid Blyton's *Secret Seven.* Again, most of the books come from the class library, reinforcing the point made by Frank Whitehead and his team in the Schools Council Project *Children and their*

Jane

Date	Title and author of book	Source	No. of pages read	No. of times read	Comment
11.9.78	Robin Hood edward B	Home	155/155	2 (2year)	It was very in- teresting. Lost of action
16.9.78	little Boy Lost	class Library	5/216	1st Time	I did not enjoy this Book. Brong
9/10/78	water Babies e Kigstey	class Library	6/150	1st time	I would like to read it but it is to hard
8/1/79	Lite house on the parime Wildér	class Library class	175/175	1st Time	a good Book and I would like to read the next Book
28/2/79	Angry river R Bomd	Library	70/70	2nd Time	it is ok But can get Boury
20/4/79	Fantastic mr #Fox	class Library	Don't kwon	1st Time	this is my frist Time and Have not finist it yet

Nicola

Date	Title and author of book	Source	No. of pages read	No. of times read / I read primary	Comment
Sept '78	Avalanche Van der loft	class Library	180/180	2/3	Quite a good book gets you envolved
Sept '78	The Cay Theodore Taylor	class Library	140/150	1/3	You dont get very Interested very
Sept '78	Felica the critic Ellen Conford	class Library	112/112	1	The book wasant very Interesting
October '78	Little boy lost M Laski	class Library	9/75	0	Not very good, you can't get very envolved
October '78	Charlottes web E B white	class Library	175/175	2 primary 3	excellant book recomended
October '78	The Intruder J.R Townsend	school library	150/150	1/3	Quite an exciting book
Decem '78	The Night Watchman Helan Cressell	school library	50/55	1/3	you can't get very interested in it
Decem '78	Bakers Dozen Leon Garfield	class library	9/58	0	you can't get envolved
January '79	Dinky Hooter Shoots Back M G Kerr	class library	50/50	1/2	a book for children under 13 yrs
January '79	The eighteenth emergency B Bryas	class library	9/163	0	It was a silly book Not good
Feb '79	silly verse - S. Milligan	class library	39/40	1	good book, laughter envolved
Feb '79	Mouse and his child E.R.Hoban	class library	173/174	1	very good book indeed
Feb '79	House of wings B. Byars	class library	110/116	1	Not a very good book
March '79	Boy Dominic	class library	125/125	home 4	an excellant book indeed
March '79	secret seven enid Blyton	home	90/90	5	Very Interesting book
April '79	Fantastic Mr fox ROALD DAHL	class Library	13/78	1	not very good
June '79	Grease. Ron de christoford	class Library	200	1	very exciting book

Books, that the provision made by the school is for many children the critical factor in the quality and quantity of their reading.

Gaining a Full Picture of a Child's Reading Ability

The five systems of assessment mentioned will each tell us something about a child's reading. Any one of them on its own gives only a partial picture. Even if we use all five of them, we do not necessarily gain a full insight into the children's reading unless we are careful. It is the interpretation of the information that produces the valuable assessment.

If children are to become fully effective readers, we need to insure that they develop the necessary habits and skills. So that in assessing a child's progress in reading, we need to pay attention particularly to five areas:

1 Recognition of the written form.

2 Understanding.

3 Enjoyment.

4 Commitment.

5 Reading experience.

1 Recognition of the Written Form The readers' ability to recognize the written forms of words they already know and to make sense of unfamiliar ones when they meet them in print.

2 Understanding The reader's ability to understand words, sentences and texts.

at the level of separate words, the reader needs to know what each word means.

but words carry different meanings in different contexts. So the level of sentence meaning is what determines the immediate meaning. For example, "funny" would suggest the meaning "amusing" at word level; but in the sentence from "My Cat" (*Breakthrough Red Book*): "He looks at our bird in a funny way," it has a subtler meaning, because of the fuller context.

the text is the whole stretch of written language that is under consideration—the chapter or the book. Because of the accumulation of meaning that is involved in reading a whole story, individual meanings change, influenced by expectation and memory. At this level "meaning" is less to do with individual words, and more to do with a total response to what is being read. When children can understand texts, it is safe to assume they have an adequate understanding of words.

An illustration of the whole process of understanding in a short example is to be found in jokes. Puns and verbal jokes depend often on shifts of meaning at sentence level, where the expected meaning is inverted or altered. A child may understand the meaning of each separate word, but not understand the point of the joke, because its meaning operates at the level of text. The sort of joke that can puzzle younger children is this:

Q. What did Tarzan say when he saw a herd of wild elephants wearing dark glasses come thundering over the horizon towards him?

A. He didn't say anything: he didn't recognize them.

3 Enjoyment Enjoyment is a very general term which implies that the reader gains some satisfaction from reading that can't be gained in any other way. Readers enjoy books, and make use of what they read. The "use" may be direct—they may have learned how to identify moths, or bake cakes, or repair bicycles; or it may be quite personal—a reader may, because of reading a story, be better able to cope with some private experience.

4 Commitment A commitment to reading implies that children will become autonomous readers, and will remain so in the future. They should want to read, not just because we make them, but because they have learned for themselves the satisfactions that reading can give. If they do not read voluntarily outside our reading lessons, then our teaching has been only partially successful.

5 Reading Experience Reading habits are established during a child's primary years. Schools need to encourage children to develop a taste for different kinds of reading, and to do this successfully, teachers need to know what children are reading as they move through the school. By encouraging pupils to sample a variety of books, and by guiding them to consider diverse authors and interests, teachers can help to develop mature readers.

Keeping Records

In general what needs to be recorded is:

Books which have been read to the child.

What other books, apart from basal series books, have been read.

Reading patterns outside school, if that is possible (find out from discussion with parents).

What areas of difficulty the child has; for example, being able to read words aloud but without understanding them.

Kinds of reading enjoyed, for instance, which stories were particularly liked, and what topics he or she is interested in.

The amount of interest shown in reading in general.

The pace of reading in different situations, for instance, it may be that a child reads stories fluently, but information books haltingly.

The difference in the child's understanding when reading silently or reading aloud. Reading aloud slows down the process and stresses individual words, whereas to read with understanding, one must grasp longer units than individual words.

Observation of the child reading and selecting books.

To illustrate approaches to the assessment of reading, here are two examples of records. The records are of two British students, John and David. John is in the equivalent of third grade and David is just completing sixth grade. Next year he will start secondary school.

John's record shows the books he read between the ages of 5 and 7 in the "infants," comments on him written by his teacher (filled in once a term) and the books he has read so far in the "juniors." You will notice how the profile created for John is a total one, in which many different kinds of information are brought together.

JOHN—Books read during the three infant years

Own sentence books
The Beach
My Story
I fell over—Breakthrough
Crocodiles are Dangerous—Bt
Who's scared of the dark—Bt
Green Eggs and Ham—Dr. Seuss
Three Billy Goats Gruff
Old Hat, New Hat—Dr. Seuss
Foot Book—Dr. Seuss
Reading own books and tapes about Timmy
Little Red Hen
Gingerbread Boy
Rr
Tt
The Mad Skipping Cat
The New House

Green Eggs and Ham
Monster goes to the Museum
Cats
Black Pirate
The Three Pirates
Roderick the Red
The Enormous Turnip
Three Little Pigs
The Monkey and the Bananas
Drakesbill
The Blue Pirate Sails
Roderick the Red
Mr Bump

Books read—Juniors

Mike Mulligan and His Steam Shovel
The Farmer (his tray is always full of farming books)
Book of Witches
The Snowman
Where the Wild Things Are
Silver Book 3 (he reread this)
House of Wings (home to read)
Watership Down (ordered thro' Puffin Club after seeing film.
    Dad reads it to him at night)
Gumdrop finds a friend
Desmond goes to New York—Althea
The Lorax—Dr. Seuss
The Pirate and the Merking
The Things you can Think—Dr. Seuss
Summer (Berenstain)
Book of Wizards

Autumn Term
John has been reading farming books. He tells me he reads the *Farmer's Weekly* at home. John has been very impressed with *The Snowman* (Raymond Briggs). He finds it hard to tell stories—when he talked about going to a farming show, what he said was purely descriptive about the stands, etc. It didn't come out in story form at all.

Spring Term
Interesting pattern of reading. At school he reads farming books and story books—mainly with pictures—but what has really grabbed him is *Watership Down*. He saw the film and

liked it. He has borrowed the cartoon book from the school library and he spends hours with that. At home his dad is reading him the real book, and John says that the following morning he goes over by himself what his dad read to him the night before. He has been very disturbed as to why Hazel was made the leader and not Bigwig. It worries him, of course, because he's very aggressive toward other children and lashes out in temper, so he thinks that you get to be Boss by being tough and aggressive. But Hazel isn't like that. John actually wrote to Richard Adams for an answer. The author wrote back and said he couldn't answer that in words, but John would understand when he was older, and then he would also understand the point of the book. That was a very hard answer to give him, and I'm not sure if it's right, but John is beginning to work it out on his own. He said recently, "I think Hazel was the leader because he had all the ideas."

John sees himself as a real writer. Everything he does is for real—writing to Richard Adams, writing farming information for his dad, labelling parts of tractors, etc. He's developing a real control over writing.

G—, the remedial team person tested John recently. On the NFFR Reading Test BC his reading age was 6.6 (chronological age 8.1).

David is 11 and his reading record might well be a useful document to pass on to his secondary school. The teacher uses many of the systems outlined above to structure her comments. Again what is produced is a detailed profile of David's reading behavior, rather than a narrow set of scores.

DAVID—Summer Term
Books read to the class
The Lion, the Witch and the Wardrobe, C. S. Lewis
I am David, Ann Holm

Books read in school (own choice)
The Magician's Nephew, C. S. Lewis
Five Children and It, E. Nesbit

Reading at home (recorded by David, but added to by parents)
The Mystery of the Fiery Eye (The Three Investigators)
Bobby Brewster's Scarecrow, H. E. Todd
Gentleman Jim, Raymond Briggs
The Puffin Book of Improbable Records (Quentin Blake and John Yeoman
Hurray for BC! (comic strip book)

Collins Guide to the Seashore
Hamlyn Guide to Shells of the World
Favorite books—*I am David* ("because of the name"!) *Mystery of the Fiery Eye* and other "Three Investigator" books.

Likes "proper books" about birds, seashore life, shells, etc.—books that *classify*. Doesn't like children's versions: says he can't find what he wants in them.

Very interested in reading but needs silence round him to read. Prefers to read in bed—parents say he always reads "for an hour before he can go to sleep."

Generally fluent reader, but he is sometimes puzzled by Math cards. When he reads aloud, he reads quickly and in a mumble, without expression.

He gets tense and visibly relaxes when he's finished.

Scored 13.5 on Schonell WRT; but didn't understand most of the words in the last three lines he read.

When he chooses books, he goes for series, with lots of books by the same author; or ones he's heard in class; or books I've mentioned.

Basic Principles for Evaluating Reading

1 The global activity called "reading" includes a range of different activities. Some of these are:

silent reading.

reading aloud.

looking for information.

browsing.

reading parts of books or other reading material.

choosing books for oneself.

understanding what one reads.

Standardized tests can only evaluate a small part of this global activity, and each test assesses a different small part. No test can assess the global activity itself; only sustained observation can do that.

2 Evaluation is a way of identifying children's *strengths*, and helping them to develop those strengths further. Systems of evaluation which only indicate weakness and failure are not helpful to either teacher or pupil.

3 Evaluation should not fracture the normal classroom environment, but should be a natural extension of it. It is a way of looking at what is already happening. All teachers naturally evaluate all the time, but most undervalue their own insights and observations, and feel they are less reliable than standardized tests.

Addresses

1 American Library
   Association
   50 East Huron Street
   Chicago, Illinois 60611

2 The Children's Book Council,
   Inc.
   67 Irving Place
   New York, New York 10003

3 Council on Interracial Books
   for Children, Inc.
   1841 Broadway
   New York, New York 10023

4 Horn Book, Inc.
   Park Square Building
   31 St. James Avenue
   Boston, Massachusetts 02116

5 Information Center on Children's Cultures
   US Committee for UNICEF
   331 East 38th Street
   New York, New York 10016

6 International Board on
   Books for Young People
   Leonhardsgraben 38a
   4051 Basel
   Switzerland

7 International Reading
   Association
   800 Barksdale Road
   P.O. Box 8139
   Newark, Delaware 19714

8 National Council of Teachers
   of English
   1111 Kenyon Road
   Urbana, Illinois 61801

9 Weston Woods
   Weston, Connecticut 06883

Further Reading

A comprehensive bibliography of books about reading and teaching reading would fill hundreds of pages: selecting a representative collection would raise more questions than it would answer, and would probably be useless to most readers. But we have been urged to include some suggestions for further reading. What follows, then, is a list of books grouped under the chapter headings. In each case, we note a few books which may be of interest and use for those who want to know a little more about the area. We make no pretense that the list is comprehensive.

We considered including a chapter on the reading-writing connection, but this was felt to be beyond the scope of the present book. Those readers interested in exploring this connection will find a list of relevant books on p. 116.

1 *The teaching of reading*
Clay, M. M. (1972) *Reading: the Patterning of Complex Behaviour.* Heinemann Educational Books.

Bussis, A. M. (December, 1982) "Burn it at the casket: Research, reading instruction, and children's learning of the first R." *Phi Delta Kappan,* 60:1, 237–241.

Cochrane, O., Cochrane, D., Scalena, S., Buchanan, E. (1984) *Reading, Writing, and Caring.* Winnipeg: Whole Language Consultants Ltd.

Donaldson, Margaret (1978) *Children's minds.* W. W. Norton & Co.

Hall, M. A. (1981) *Teaching Reading as a Language Experience.* Merrill.

McCracken, M. J., & McCracken, R. A. (1979) *Reading, Writing, and Language: A practical guide for primary teachers.* Winnipeg: Peguis Publishers Ltd.

Holdaway, D. (1979) *The Foundations of Literacy.* Scholastic.

Goodman, K. and Y. (1973) "The Analysis of oral reading miscues," in *Psycholinguistics and Reading.* Smith, F. (ed.). Holt, Rinehart & Winston.

Lunzer, E. and Gardner, K. (1979) *The Effective Use of Reading.* Heinemann Educational Books.

Rosen, C. and H. (1973) *The Language of Primary School Children.* Penguin Education.

Rosen, H. (1985) *Stories and Meanings*. London: National Association of Teachers of English.

Sherman, B. (November 1979) "Reading for meaning." *Learning*, 60:1, 41–44.

Southgate, V. *et al.* (1981) *Extending Beginning Reading*. Heinemann Educational Books.

Smith, F. (1971) *Understanding Reading*. Holt, Rinehart & Winston.

————. (1979) *Reading Without Nonsense*. Teachers College Press.

————. (1983) *Essays into Literacy*. Heinemann Educational Books.

2 *Involving parents with reading*
Baghban, M. (1984) *Our Daughter Learns to Read and Write: A case study from birth to three*. The International Reading Association.

Bissex, G. L. (1980) *Gnys at Wrk: A child learns to write and read*. Harvard University Press.

Butler, D. (1980) *Babies Need Books*. Atheneum

Butler, D., and Clay, M. M. (1979) *Reading Begins at Home*. Heinemann Educational Books.

Ferreiro, E., and Teberosky, A. (1982) *Literacy Before Schooling*. Heinemann Educational Books.

Meek, M. (1982) *Learning to Read*. Bodley Head.

Monson, Dianne L., and McClenathan, DayAnn K. (eds.) (1979) *Developing Active Readers: Ideas for Parents, Teachers, and Librarians*. The International Reading Association.

Rhodes, L., and Hill, M. (1983) "Home-school cooperation in integrated language arts programs." In B. Busching and J. Schwartz (Eds.), *Integrating the Language Arts in the Elementary School*. National Council of Teachers of English, p. 179–188.

Taylor, Bev, and Johns, Jerry. (1983) *Teach Me to Read! A Booklet for Parents and Teachers*. Parents and Reading Committee of the Illinois Reading Council.

Taylor, Denny. (1983) *Family Literacy. Young Children Learning to Read and Write*. Heinemann Educational Books.

3 *A prereading program*
Clark, M. M. (1976) *Young Fluent Readers*. Heinemann Educational Books.

DES (1975) *A Language for Life* (The Bullock Report). HMSO.

Goodman, K. S., & Goodman, Y. M. (1979) Learning to Read is Natural. In L. B. Resnick & P. A. Weaver (Eds.), *Theory and Practice of Early Reading* (Volume 2). Erlbaum.

Heath, S. B. (1981) *Ways with Words: Ethnography of communication, communities and classrooms.* Cambridge University Press.

Linfors, J. W. (1980) *Children's Language and Learning.* Prentice-Hall.

Wells, G. (1981). *Learning Through Interaction: The study of language development.* Cambridge University Press.

4 *Organizing a reading program*

Barnes, D. (1975) *From Communication to Curriculum.* Penguin Books.

DeFord, D. E. (September, 1981) "Literacy: Reading, writing and other essentials." *Language Arts,* 58: 6, 652–658.

Eisner, E. W. (1982) *Cognition and Curriculum: A basis for deciding what to teach.* Longman.

MacKay, D., Schaub P., and Thompson B. (1978) *Breakthrough to Literacy: Teachers' Manual. Illustrated edition.* Longman.

Milz, V. (1980) "The comprehension-centered classroom: Setting it up and making it work" (Videotape). In D. J. Strickler (Producer & Director), Reading comprehension: An instructional videotape series. Bloomington, IN: 211 Education Building, Indiana University.

Moon, C. (1977) *Individualized Reading.* University of Reading, Reading Centre.

Rhodes, L. K. (1983) "Organizing the elementary classroom for effective language learning." In U. H. Hardt (Ed.), *Teaching Reading with the Other Language Arts.* International Reading Association.

5 *Choosing books for children and helping children to choose*

Christensen, J. (Chair) (1983) *Your Reading: A booklist for junior high and middle school students.* National Council of Teachers of English.

Cullinan, Bernice E.; Karrer, Mary K.; and Pillar, Arlene M. (1981) *Literature and the Child.* Harcourt Brace Jovanovich.

Neville, M. H., and Pugh, A. K. (1982) *Towards Independent Reading.* Heinemann Educational Books.

Open University (1982) *Children, Language and Literature.* Open University Press.

Rhodes, L. K. (February, 1981) "I can read! Predictable books as resources for reading and writing instruction." *Reading Teacher,* 34:6, 511–518.

Sims, Rudine. (1982) *Shadow and Substance: Afro-American Experience in Contemporary Children's Fiction.* National Council of Teachers of English.

Spencer, M. (1976) "Stories are for telling" *English in Education* 10(3).

Whitehead, F. S. *et al.* (1977) *Children and Their Books.* Macmillan Educational.

a) *Bias and stereotyping in general*
Dixon, B. (1977) *Catching Them Young* (2 vols). Pluto.

b) *Books on racial bias*
Baker, Augusta. (1975) "The Changing Image of the Black in Children's Literature" *The Horn Book* 51(February 1975), 79–88.

Council on Interracial Books for Children. 1980 *Guidelines for Selecting Bias-free Textbooks and Storybooks.* CIBC.

Eliminating Stereotypes, School Division Guidelines. 1981 Houghton Mifflin.

Rollock, Barbara. 1979 *The Black Experience in Children's Books.* New York Public Library.

c) *Books on Sexism*
Egoff, Sheila, G. T. Stubbs, and Z. F. Ashley. 1980 *Only Connect.* Oxford University Press.

Rupley, William, Jesus Garcia, and Bonnie Longnion. 1981 "Sex Role Portrayal in Reading Materials: Implications for the 1980s," *The Reading Teacher* 34(April 1981), 786–91.

Sheridan, Marcia E., editor. 1982 Sex Stereotypes and Reading: Research and Strategies. International Reading Association.

Women on Words and Images. 1972 *Dick and Jane as Victims: Sex Stereotyping in Children's Readers.* Carolingian.

6 *Introducing children to literature*
Coody, Betty. (1983) *Using Literature with Young Children.* 3rd ed. William C. Brown.

Hearne, Betsy. (1981) *Choosing Books for Children: A Commonsense Guide.* Delacorte Press.

Ingham, J. (1981) *Books and Reading Development.* Heinemann Educational Books.

Kimmel, Margaret Mary, and Segel, Elizabeth. (1983) *For Reading Out Loud!: A Guide to Sharing Books With Children.* Delacorte Press.

Paulin, Mary Ann. (1982) *Creative Uses of Children's Literature.* The Shoestring Press.

Sims, R. (1980) "Children's literature in a comprehension-centered reading program" (Videotape). In D. J. Strick le (Director & Producer), Reading comprehension: An instructional videotape series. Distributed by Heinemann Educational Books.

Trelease, J. (1983) *The Read-aloud Handbook*. Penguin Books.

7 *Reading for meaning*

Britton, J. (1984) *English Teaching: An international exchange*. Portsmouth, NH: Heinemann Educational Books.

Flood, J. (Ed.) (1984) *Promoting Reading Comprehension*. International Reading Association.

Goodman, K. S. (1984) "Unity in reading." In A. C. Purves & O. Niles (Eds.), *Becoming Readers in a Complex society*: 83rd Yearbook of the National Society for the Study of Education (Part 1). University of Chicago Press.

Goodman, Y., & Burke, C. (1980) "A reading curriculum: Focus on comprehension." *Reaching Strategies: Focus on comprehension*. Holt, Rinehart & Winston.

Halliday, M. A. K. (1975) *Learning How to Mean: Foundations of Language and Development*. Vol. 1, ed. Eric Lenneberg and Elizabeth Lenneberg. Academic Press.

Harste, J. C. (Host & Developer), & Jurewicz, E. (Producer & Director). (1985). The Authoring Cycle: Read better, write better, reason better (Videotape Series). Heinemann Educational Books.

Harste, J. C., Woodward, V. A., & Burke, C. L. (1984) *Language Stories and Literacy Lessons*. Heinemann Educational Books.

Lunzer, E. *et al.* (1979) *The Effective Use of Reading*. Heinemann Educational Books.

National Assessment of Educational Progress. (1981) *Reading, Thinking, and Writing: Results from the 1979–80 National Assessment of Reading and Literature*. National Education Commission for the States.

Rosenblatt, L. (1982). *The Reader, the Text, the Poem*. Southern University Press.

8 *The librarian and the reading program*

Chambers, Aidan. (1977) *Introducing Books to Children*. Heinemann Educational Books.

Children's Book Council, eds. (1981) *Children's Books: Awards and Prizes*. The Children's Book Council.

Getting Started: A Bibliography of Ideas and Procedures. (1983) International Association for School Librarianship.

Hearne, Betsy. (1981) *Choosing Books for Children: A Commonsense Guide*. Delacorte Press.

Helping Children Learn About Reading. (1983) National Association for the Education of Young Children.

Kimmel, Margaret Mary and Segel, Elizabeth. (1983) *For Reading Out Loud!* Delacorte Press.

Pellowski, Anne. (1977) *The World of Storytelling.* Bowker.

Sharing: A Challenge for All. Proceedings from the Eleventh IASL Annual Conference. (1983) International Association for School Librarianship.

Spirt, Diana L. (1978) *Introducing More Books: A Guide for the Middle Grades.* Bowker.

Thomas, James L. (1980) *Using Periodicals in School Library Media Centers: Resources and Activities.* T. S. Denison.

Trelease, Jim. (1982) *The Read-Aloud Handbook.* Penguin Books.

Tway, Eileen, ed. (1981) *Reading Ladders for Human Relations.* 6th ed. National Council of Teachers of English.

Weisburg, Hilda K. and Toor, Ruth. (1979) *Elementary School Librarian's Almanac.* The Center for Applied Research in Education.

White, Mary Lou, ed. (1981) *Adventuring with Books: A Booklist for Pre-K–Grade 6.* National Council of Teachers of English.

Yonkers Public Library Children's Services. (1979) *A Guide to Subjects & Concepts in Picture Book Format.* 2d ed. Oceana Publications.

9 *Reference and study skills*
Atwell, M., Block, J., & Modesatt, M. (1983) *Learning in College: Integrating Information.* Kendall Hunt.

Bransford, J. D., & Stein, B.S. (1984) *The Ideal Problem Solver.* W. H. Freeman.

10 *Assessing progress in reading*
Cunningham, P. W. (1982) "Diagnosis by Observation." In *Approaches to the Informal Evaluation of Reading*, ed. J. J. Pikulski and T. Shanahan. The International Reading Association.

Fagan, W. T.; Cooper, C. R.; and Jensen, J. M. (1975) *Measures for Research and Evaluation in the English Language Arts.* National Council of Teachers of English.

Goodman, Y. (1978) "Kid watching: An alternative to testing." *Journal of National Elementary School Principals*, 57:4, 22–27.

Goodman, Y. M., & Burke, C. L. (1972) *Reading Miscue Inventory.* Macmillan.

Gorman, T. *et al.* (1981) *Language Performance in Schools. Primary Survey Report* (1). HMSO.

Jaggar, A., & Smith-Burke, T. (1985) *Observing the Language Learner*. National Council of Teachers of English.

McCaig, R. (1981) "A District-Wide Plan for the Evaluation of Student Writing." In *Perspectives on Writing in Grades 1–8*, ed. Shirley Haley-James. National Council of Teachers of English.

Stibbs, A. (1980) *Assessing Children's Language*. Boynton/Cook.

Venezky, R. L. (1974) *Testing in Reading: Assessment and Instructional Decision Making*. National Council of Teachers of English.

Reading and writing connections
Britton, J.; Burgess, T.; Martin, A.; and Rosen, H. (1975) *The Development of Writing Abilities, 11–18*. Macmillan.

Burrows, Alvina Treut; Jackson, Doris C.; and Saunders, Dorothy O. (1984) *They All Want to Write*, 4th ed. The Shoestring Press.

Chomsky, Carol. (1979) "Approaching Reading Through Invented Spelling." In *Theory and Practice of Early Reading*, Vol. 2, ed. L. B. Resnick and P. A. Weaver. Lawrence Erlbaum. Pp. 43–65.

Evanechko, P.; Ollila, L.; and Armstrong, R. (1974) "An Investigation of the Relationship Between Children's Performance in Written Language and Their Reading Ability." RESEARCH IN THE TEACHING OF ENGLISH 8: 315–26.

Graves, Donald. (1983) *Writing: Teachers & Children at Work*. Heinemann Educational Books.

Hennings, Dorothy G. (1978) *Communication in Action*. Rand McNally.

Myers, Miles and Gray, James, eds. (1983) *Theory and Practice in the Teaching of Composition: Processing, Distancing, and Modeling*. National Council of Teachers of English.

Newkirk, Thomas and Atwell, Nancie, eds. (1982) *Understanding Writing: Ways of Observing, Learning and Teaching*. The Northeast Regional Exchange.

Petty, Walter T. (1978) "The Writing of Young Children." In *Research on Composing*, ed. Charles R. Cooper and Lee Odell. National Council of Teachers of English.

Robinson, K. (1980) "Drama, Theatre and Social Reality.' In *Exploring Theatre and Education*, ed. K. Robinson. Heinemann.

Smith, Frank. (1982) *Writing and the Writer*. Heinemann.

Smith, R.: Jensen, K.: and Dillingofski, M. (1971) "The Effects of Integrating Reading and Writing on Four Variables." *Research in the Teaching of English* 5:179–89.

Stewig, John Warren. (1980) *Read to Write*. Holt, Rinehart, and Winston.

Turbill, J., ed. (1982) *No Better Way to Teach Writing!* Heinemann Educational Books.

Walsh, R. D., ed. (1982) *"Children Want to Write . . .": Donald Graves in Australia.* Heinemann Educational Books.

Index